# PUBLIC SPEAKING

Learn How to Negotiate and Master the Secrets of Crucial Conversation for Effective Leadership

(Smart Ways to Get the Attention of Your Audience)

Akash King

Published by Rob Miles

© Akash King

All Rights Reserved

*Public Speaking: Learn How to Negotiate and Master the Secrets of Crucial Conversation for Effective Leadership (Smart Ways to Get the Attention of Your Audience)*

ISBN 978-1-989990-15-5

All rights reserved. No part of this guide may be reproduced in any form without permission in writing from the publisher except in the case of brief quotations embodied in critical articles or reviews.

**Legal & Disclaimer**

The information contained in this book is not designed to replace or take the place of any form of medicine or professional medical advice. The information in this book has been provided for educational and entertainment purposes only.

The information contained in this book has been compiled from sources deemed reliable, and it is accurate to the best of the Author's knowledge; however, the Author cannot guarantee its accuracy and validity and cannot be held liable for any errors or omissions. Changes are periodically made to this book. You must consult your doctor or get professional medical advice before using any of the suggested remedies, techniques, or information in this book.

Upon using the information contained in this book, you agree to hold harmless the Author from and against any damages, costs, and expenses, including any legal fees potentially resulting from the application of any of the information provided by this guide. This disclaimer applies to any damages or injury caused by the use and application, whether directly or indirectly, of any advice or information presented, whether for breach of contract, tort, negligence, personal injury, criminal intent, or under any other cause of action.

You agree to accept all risks of using the information presented inside this book. You need to consult a professional medical practitioner in order to ensure you are both able and healthy enough to participate in this program.

# Table of Contents

INTRODUCTION .................................................................. 1

CHAPTER 1: PUBLIC SPEAKING IS EASY ONCE YOU KNOW HOW .............................................................................. 4

CHAPTER 2: DISCOVERING YOUR STORY AND LEARNING HOW TO TELL IT ............................................................... 16

CHAPTER 3: ANALYZING YOUR AUDIENCE ....................... 23

CHAPTER 4: THE ESSENTIAL QUALITIES OF A PUBLIC SPEAKER ........................................................................... 31

CHAPTER 5: BUT I DON'T WANT TO BE A PUBLIC SPEAKER ........................................................................................... 38

CHAPTER 6: COLLECTING NUGGETS OF CONFIDENCE ....... 46

CHAPTER 7: HOW CREATIVE VISUALIZATION WORKS ...... 54

CHAPTER 8: FOUR QUESTIONS ABOUT LEADERSHIP ........ 60

CHAPTER 9: TO CONTROL FEAR YOU NEED TO UNDERSTAND FEAR ......................................................... 67

CHAPTER 10: GENERAL TIPS FOR PUBLIC SPEAKING ........ 78

CHAPTER 11: NARROWING DOWN YOUR SUBJECT .......... 84

CHAPTER 12: BECOMING LARGER THAN LIFE.................... 87

CHAPTER 13: THE BENEFITS OF PUBLIC SPEAKING............ 99

CHAPTER 14: COURAGE AND CONFIDENCE..................... 118

CHAPTER 15: THE BREAKTHROUGH ............................... 126

CHAPTER 16: WEAR YOUR HEART ON YOUR SLEEVE....... 131

CHAPTER 17: IT'S NOT WHAT YOU SAY........................... 135

CHAPTER 18: HOW TO FIND THE MESSAGE .................... 142

CHAPTER 19: USING SLIDES, IMAGES AND POWERPOINT ................................................................................. 152

CHAPTER 20: EVALUATION............................................. 158

CHAPTER 21: WHO IS THE BEST PERSON TO ORGANIZE YOUR SPEAKING BUSINESS?........................................... 171

CONCLUSION................................................................ 178

## Introduction

Fear of public speaking is a common fear and is a source of anxiety and stress for many people all over the world. Some people consider this to be the most trivial of all fears, but it is estimated that 75% of all speakers experience some degree of anxiety or nervousness when speaking in public, whether it be in front of a small or a large group.So, if like so many people, you are fearful of speaking in public, then be assured this no longer needs to be a problem. Speaking before a group or crowd need not be a stressful experience. This is because as social beings, needing to interact with each other, we have developed a variety of techniques to help us cope with this fear and to overcome it.

I was inspired to write this E-Guide while I was searching for material to help me with my own fear of speaking in public. As a mature student studying in college, I felt much anxiety, as I had to deliver a presentation in front of the class. The tips and techniques contained in these pages were very helpful to me. Putting the information into practice helped me immensely, by turning what would otherwise have been a very stressful situation into a positive experience. I was able to deal with my fear of speaking in public, which enabled me to deliver my presentation with a marked degree of confidence. These days, I am no longer plagued by the fear of speaking in public: in the past, the mere thought of public speaking was enough to make me feel fearful. So, whether you wish to say a few words at a best friend's wedding, at a family gathering, or to speak in a formal or professional capacity, I hope the information contained in the following pages will assist you in overcoming any fears you may have of speaking in public. And best of all, you will discover there are many things that you can do on your own without having to spend countless amounts of money.

## Chapter 1: Public Speaking Is Easy Once You Know How

Public Speaking is so easy, once you know how – that's all you need – you just need to know how, you can do it!

Public speaking is 80% mental attitude! 20% is the actual delivery!

What is going on in your mind as it relates to your being an effective, winning public speaker?

Let's take a look!Read an actual incident below:

I had a university student, we will call Sabrina, in one of my classes and she was deathly afraid of making presentations during the class times.

She would see me on campus outside of class and confess that she could not do the speaking assignments set for her and the group.She was self-conscious, nervous, spoke like a mouse at the beginning; she had incorrect pronunciations, incorrect posture, poor eye contact, everything that would make her in total, a poor speaker in public.

Isimplywouldadviseher,tofollowthe steps, I am about to share with you and she would be fine, I had faith in her!At the end of the semester I am proud to say that she was the most improved student in the group.She was so successful, that she admitted that she now took on new responsibilities at her job; responsibilities that she had been resisting, because she thought she was not able to representherselfwellinpublicpresentations on behalf of her organization.

How did she overcome?She, like the rest of the group, started by identifying their individual fears of public speaking!

# What are your

# public speaking fears?

FIRST STEP – IDENTIFY YOUR FEARS

What are your particular fears about speaking in public?Write them down.You may print this page to do so or simply have a note pad ready.Write as many as you wish.If it is only one, jot it down so you can see it clearly:

List them:

Fear of

Fear of

Fear of

Fear of

Once you have listed your fears let us take a look at the following scenario; write down what your response would be to the following:

CASE: You are invited to give a short speech to a group of overseas visitors about your organization without notice.How do you react to such a request?

Now that you have listed your fears, we are now ready to analyze them!

You have written down what you would do in the above scenario, let us examine why you would respond in the way you would.Is it because you are confident and ready to speak why you would take on the challenge, or is it because you dread speaking in public that you would not take on the challenge? Maybe you would take on the challenge but lack the full comfort and confidence you would love to have in carrying out such a relatively simple task….if so, good – at least you are willing to try!

FEAR OF SPEAKING IN PUBLIC

Fear of public speaking is real for many persons. In the event they must do this, they simply "break into a cold sweat" at the thought of having to express themselves in open arena. A quick survey of a class of tertiary students revealed some of the fears some people may have:-

Fear of appearing foolish
Fear of being boring
Fear of being criticized
Fear of being misunderstood
Fear of being scrutinized
Fear of fear
Fear of forgetting the speech

Fear of losing your audience
Fear of losing your train of thought
Fear of making mistakes
Fear of mispronunciation
Fear of speaking too long
Fear of speaking too much
Fear of speaking too quickly
Fear of speaking too slowly
Fear of using the wrong words

Did you write any of the above fears?

Even Moses the great Hebrew leader, when called to mobilize the Israelites to make the exodus out of Egypt had his own fears of public speaking, as is documented in his reply to the Lord, "O, my Lord, I have never been eloquent… but I am slow of speech and slow of tongue." (Exodus 4:10; NRSV). This was of course addressed when the Lord appointed his brother Aaron to speak for him.

It is not true that in all cases where we are called upon to speak in public do we have someone to speak for us.**Preparation,**

**Preparation, Practice and Practice** are the keys to overcoming these fears.

Now that you have written down your fears and you may have matched some of them with what you note the list above, you may now realize that specific fears in Public Speaking are all very common. Each fear can be overcome.

Effective Public Speaking comes as a result of addressing fears and laying them to rest. This requires more than facing your fears and doing the thing you fear most. That alone will not help.

Preparation not only means to prepare your speech, it means preparing your mind, body and soul! Practice not only means a rehearsal of your script but it means being in a constant of awareness of yourself as a public speaker – any time of day or night. You not only speak in public at a podium, when giving an address, you speak in public when you are having a conversation in the hallway during your coffee break– or how you speak to the bank teller whilst doing your banking transactions.

Where Do Fears Have Their Origin? Where Did Your Fear Of Public Speaking Begin?

Fear of public speaking has an origin; think about it….when did **your** particular fears develop?

Have you noticed how you yourself have criticized speakers in the past? What is it that you did not like about a particular speech or speaker?Did your fear develop while in school and your fellow students would laugh at you when you had something to say? Or was it that you were told unkind things as a child, and these things are still residing in your consciousness or subconscious?

To answer these questions I need you to do another exercise that will help you along this journey of self-discovery as a public speaker.

Do this exercise before reading further, it benefits you better!

A DRAWING EXERCISE

STEP 1

Draw a picture of yourself when you were ten years old. Use a pencil. If you wish you may colour your picture with markers or crayons. It does not have to be a Picasso drawing; it could even be a stick drawing.

STEP 2

List 3 adjectives that described you at that time – positive or negative – what you heard about yourself from others or what you thought about yourself or both.

STEP 3

List the names you were called by your friends, family or relatives – nick names or pet names.

What does My 10 year-old Self have to do with Public Speaking?

Now you may wonder 'what does drawing a picture of myself, at ten years old, have to do with public speaking?' I always answer my students – it has everything to do with public speaking. If you listed as one of your fears 'being scrutinized' or 'having people look at you', or 'being the centre of attention', or 'being criticized', you will begin to realize that it has everything to do with public speaking.

When you are speaking to a group of people you become the focus of their attention. They are not only hearing your voice, but they are looking at your clothes, your face, your hair, your mouth, and your teeth! That is some serious scrutiny. As a member of an audience, you have scrutinized speakers, haven't you? When you look at what stands out in your adult mind about your 10 year-old self, does it make you happy, bringing back fond memories? Or does it cause angst to stir up inside of you? Do you feel nonchalant? Do you feel rejected? Not a part of the crowd? Do you feel that you have lost the spark you had when you were 10 compared to now? No matter what you are feeling, it still resides with you today! Those are the feelings that contribute to your fear of public speaking. Share your picture with a family member or friend and discuss this thoroughly.

Takealookatyourpictureagain—lookatthe clothing you drew — did you have something in your hand?Are you standing by a bike? Did you draw just your face, with no body? Did you make your picture very small or very large? If so why did you draw what you did?Ask yourself these questions and find your answers.

When you get up to speak, all your fears, hopes and dreams, get up to the microphone or lectern with you — they contribute to fears (or confidence) you experience in your mind and body!But guess what, your audience has no clue what is going on inside your mind, only you do!

The audience does not even care. In fact members of the audience wish they had the confidence that you do to speak in public!The audience has faith in you to be good!They hope not to be disappointed but really, they expect that you will be good!

So there you are at the microphoneand suddenly you become awash with heavy perspiration, rapid heartbeat, voice begins to crack, hands shake becausethefearreaction ofadrenalineflowing throughyourbody, tempts you torunoutoftherebecause feeling embarrassed is the worst thing that could happen to you!All this because of some name they called you back then or worse, how insecure you felt at that age. You feel like you are under a microscope and everyone knows your deepest darkest, insecurities, fears and secrets!

That's where the origin of fear of public speaking is!

Do you see the relationship with your 10 year-old self andwhoyouaretodayandwhatyoufearabout public speaking?Some negative programming may have even happened before (or after) 10 years old, but I just want you to recognize this fact and understand that some of your fears are based on past experiences and not necessarily with public speaking itself!

## Chapter 2: Discovering Your Story And Learning How To Tell It

Everyone has a story to tell. This is a fact. Often times, in conversations we tell ourselves that we don't have anything to contribute and that we are not interesting enough for people to want to know anything about us. These are some of the tiny lies disguised as truths we tell ourselves to validate our poor self-esteem and low confidence issues. So, when an opportunity comes to speak in public, these excuses that we make become amplified. In reality, we all have unique experiences and these experiences offer us a perspective on things that other people will not have.

Being a successful public speaker is about taking those experiences and sharing them with people. It doesn't matter if you are speaking at a press conference, a seminar for professionals or at your best friend's wedding. The purpose remains the same; to share your story. In order to share your story successfully, you must first know what that story is and then understand how to tell that story. In a few short moments, we will do both.

Discovering Your Story

I remember the first ever professional networking event I attended. It was an awkwardexperience for me from start to finish. First, you have to show up (obviously). Then next, you would go around the room introducing yourself to people. Before that event, I never really thought about what I did professionally or how I did what I did until the moment I was asked to talk about it. That evening, it seemed as though everywhere I went to in the room, people wanted to know who I was and what I did (Duh! It's a networking event). I was so poorly prepared for that event that even my business card had more to say about me than I did and the business card only had two phrases on it;

my name and my job title. I am sure you can imagine the crickets that followed me around the room. Anyway, I learned two of my biggest lessons that night;always know your own story and bow ties are not for every formal occasion.

To discover your story, you have to start by asking yourself pertinent questions. One of those questions would be, who are you? Now this question is not about discovering your place in the universe. That's a whole different ball game entirely. This is looking at your journey so far and reflecting on the key role you have played in it. For instance, would you describe yourself as a doctor or a husband? A friend or teacher? Be careful though. Because at this point, a lot of people lose it in a bid to come up with a "title" that they feel is socially prestigious and acceptable. They lose out on the authenticity of who they really are which is usually where their most impactful experiences come from. If you have played the role of a housewife for the better part of a decade and then you become a career woman for a year following that, don't pick the latter simply because it is more socially appealing. The 10 years you spent as a housewife has enriched you with experiences that form a key part in telling your story. The Career woman is just an evolution on that journey. Own your truth.

The next part of this process will be to expand on the title that you have given yourself.Think of my business card at that networking event I talked about. It won't be enough to just have the title there. You need to build on it. To expatiate on your role,the focus should be on the impactful and relevant things you have done in that capacity. This is not necessarily highlighting what you do per se, save that for your job interview. When it comes to telling your story, what matters is your experience. What you do is just a tiny part of it. The experiences that surround what you do or what you have done is what will enrich your story and give your narrative that unique perspective that people are looking for. Do this successfully and you have your story. The next step would be how to tell that story.

Learning How to Tell Your Story

In public speaking, the main thing that connects your audience with the story you are telling them is relatability. People need to be able to relate with what you are saying.They come because you have something they feel would impact them. However, always bear in mind that people have opinions and perspectives. And when they come to you, they are trying to either validate their opinion or elevate their perspective. To be able to help them do this, you would have to take them from where they are currently, to where you are. Now, you can't get to where they are if you don't try to relate with them.So, here are some tips on improving how you relate with people

Be personable. Let your words and body language be warm and inviting. When you talk, use terms that people can understand.

Pace yourself. Talking too fast or too slow will cause you to lose your audience before you even get halfway.

Don't make it about you. Yes, you are there to share your experiences with your audience. But don't focus too much on yourself. Use general perceptions about your narrative to get your story across. That way, you are starting from what they think before bringing it back to what you know.

**Task:**

Try to strike up a conversation with a random stranger that lasts at least five minutes. When you are done, go back home and take notes. In your notes, write out who you think was a dominant personality in that conversation. Then, highlight your thoughts about that interaction. If 5 minutes seem like a long time for you, start with one minute conversations and build on it from there.

These random chats with strangers would help you build your people communication skills. When you are able to talk with one stranger for at least 5 minutes and get to a point where both parties are engaged , try and see if you can grow this task to accommodate two people.

## Chapter 3: Analyzing Your Audience

One of the most important aspects of effective speech is understanding the needs of the people in the audience. If you know why your audience is there and what it expects from you, you are likely to be much more successful in your efforts as a speaker. Think about it. When you hear a speaker you often have an expectation of what you want to 'get' from his or her speech. Being able to determine what your audience wants from you may be the single most effective thing a speaker can do before speaking.

But how do you know what the audience wants? There are two main methods to analysis the needs of your audience. They are:

Demographic Analysis

Situational Analysis

Understanding your audience is one of the most crucial elements of effective communication. Audience analysis offers valuable insight about your audience, which can help you to choose and develop a relevant, meaningful topic. For a message to resonate with an audience the message must be one that is in sync with an audience's attitudes, beliefs, values and opinions.It must also be presented in language that an audience can understand and with a non-verbal message that interests them.

There are two main areas to consider when analyzing your audience: demographics and the situation of the topic. For each of these areas, there are a set of questions to answer which will help stimulate your thinking about your audience. In addition to the questions below, you should consider how each of these factors (age, socio-economic status, etc.) shapes your audience's attitudes, expectations, and opinions about you and your topic.

Demographic Analysis

Is my audience homogeneous or heterogeneous? If homogeneous, how are the readers alike? What do they have in common? If heterogeneous, how are the readers different from one another? What do readers have in common despite their differences?

What is the average age of my readers? What range of ages is represented?

In terms of socio-economic status, how would I describe my reading audience? Where do they fit in society's social and economic status?

What occupations are represented in my reading audience?

What are my readers' political and religious affiliations?

What ethic, racial and cultural groups are represented in my reading audience?

What is my role in relationship to my reading audience? Are we status equals are we of mixed status?

Situational Analysis

How much does my audience already know about my topic?

What can I inform my readers about that they do not already know? What new information would my readers benefit from? How could they use this new information?

What time of day will I be speaking?

Where will I be speaking?

Is the room comfortable for the audience?

Are audience members required to attend or did they choose to come?

What do they expect to get from my speech?

You may be wondering how you can learn about your audience before you make your speech. In a classroom setting, you are likely to have familiarity with your audience before you make one of the major presentations in the class simply because you've been in class with them.But if you are speaking to an audience outside of class, the best way to find out about your audience is to ask the person who has invited you to speak.Ask questions about their ages, gender, knowledge about your topic, and the reason that they are sitting in front of you in first place.Do they expect to learn something from you or are you more of an entertaining speaker.Is it OK if your speech takes on a persuasive tact or will that turn off your audience?These are questions that you need to ask your audience.

Once you have a clearer picture of your audience, you need to get down to the organization of your speech.A good format for setting up the organization of your speech is to ask:

What is the general purpose of my speech (inform, persuade, entertain, celebrate)

What is the specific purpose of my speech (what am I informing, persuading, entertaining or celebrating).

Audiences like to feel as though they have gotten their "money's worth" so to speak.When you write your specific purpose, offer your audience a benefit. Your specific purpose may be written like this:

After listening to my speech today, you will be well informed about the history of Cape May, New Jersey.

Another example:

After my speech today, you will be convinced that you will adopt a vegetarian lifestyle.

What is the central idea or the thesis of my speech? In other words, what do I think of this topic?

For example, you may have as your specific purpose to persuade your audience to adopt a vegetarian lifestyle. Your central idea or thesis is that by adopting a vegetarian lifestyle, your audience will be happier and healthier.

Although we cannot look into the minds of our audience to determine exactly what they want from us as speakers, there are ways to learn about your audience. They include:

Asking the person who invited you to speak
Surveying the audience in advance
Checking out your speech venue in advance
Research!
Finally, a speaker must choose message strategies that meet an audience's beliefs, attitudes, opinions, and understanding about a topic as well as their more general needs such as their values, motives, language abilities and even psychological make up. When you invest in understanding your audience, it pays off in how the audience perceives you and makes sense of your message.

Audience Analysis Exercise:
Imagine you are giving a speech on the benefits of physical fitness.
You may choose from different types of audiences:
Preschool
Middle School
High School

College Age
Senior Citizens
Choose one audience and write an introduction geared to what you think are the audience's needs.
Share it with the class!

## Chapter 4: The Essential Qualities Of A Public Speaker

There is a world of difference between a good public speaker and a great public speaker. A good public speaker gets the job done anyhow but a great public speaker gets the job done in style, with class and with a touch of finesse. You need to know what separates the children from the adults and work at incorporating them into your presentations.

**Knowledge:** A speaker can talk about anything so long as he or she knows what to say. This is not to say that professional speakers should not strive to carve a niche for themselves so that they will walk the road to becoming an authority in their line of work. Every public speaker must be knowledgeable as the essence of public speaking is in being able to add value to your listeners and this might be by making new knowledge available to them.

**Language**: The hallmark of any speaker is the ability to possess a good command of a particular language in order to be able to communicate effectively. Nowadays it is not a requirement that a public speaker should also be a polyglot that is someone who understands and possibly speaks multiple languages. Just in case you get the opportunity to speak to a people, whose language you do not understand they will most likely get you an interpreter to help translate what you say and make sure that your message reaches your intended audience.

**Charisma**: This is a natural attribute that is essential for speakers to have, as it is a necessary ingredient in the art of public speaking. It is what I would like to refer to as some indescribable magnetic force of attraction that just makes people want to listen to you. The downside of this is that, as a speaker if you rely only on charisma to pass your message across you will end up doing a shoddy job because the effective public speaker is one whose presentation is high on logic, emotion and sincerity of purpose simultaneously.

**Sincerity of purpose**: A must have for any public speaker is the ability to be be able to connect with the audience on an emotional level such that they find you believable. The unmistakable truth is that a good number of people know how to identify a phoney from the real deal, trust me I do not know how they do it but perhaps it is all in the body language signs and remember communication is essentially non verbal as far as weight is concerned. The opposite of public speaking is what I call private doing, it is not enough just to talk about issues you must also do what you tell people to do. That is how you can increase your believability level.

Without any doubt, an effective public speaker must have many more qualities than those mentioned so far because as things stand, one article alone cannot contain all of them. The bottom line is that you must and will learn from the experiences you gather and from the experiences of those around you.

It is no secret that public speaking is causing a lot of fear and stress, in fact public speaking ranks high in causing fear in many of us. The following are different methods you can use to introduce your speech in an interesting way.

Use a Bold, Straightforward Statement

There are so many bold, straightforward statements that you can use such as "good morning ladies and gentlemen, I would like you to pay full attention to my speech because I will you tell something incredibly important to your life and well being", "guys, I want you to concentrate on this presentation because things I will talk are relevant to you and beloved people", "you may not believe me, but I'm not going to begin this speech unless I have your full attention. Can I have it?" and etc.

Begin With an Appealing Promise

A promise is quite similar to the bold straightforward statement but it just gives the audience some kind of hope. With the hope, the audience members tend to listen to what you have to say more because they are promised to get something back after listening. An appealing promise could be "ladies and gentlemen, I really want you to pay attention to my speech because I'm going to elaborate to you how I protect myself from getting HIV", "you will learn how to make more money if you listen attentively to my speech", "guys, I'm going to offer a gift to anyone who can answer my question after I finish this speech. So, pay attention to get the nice gift free" and etc.

Tell a Good Joke

If you are a good joke teller, you could be one step ahead of the game because audience participants are usually excited by a very good joke, thus paying attention to the speaker and speech, usually with the hope to get more entertainment.

Anyway, if you use a joke in your introduction, ensure that it is short (as not to waste time), relevant (as not to break your audience attention from the objective of the speech, and genuine (as not to offend any person). Besides these, you should also study your audience members well before deciding to choose a joke.

Narrate a Story

A story also works well with the introduction especially when the speaker is really good at narrating it. The story could be real or made up. But the telling should take the audience as closely to the reality as possible. So, the story narrator should use different tones according to the plots and gestures to make the story seem more realistic.

Start With a Thought Provoking question or Challenge

Your audience members come to listen to you because they want to learn something. So, why don't you challenge them to learn? You can do that by asking a thought provoking question in the introduction. If the question is really interesting, they will listen to your speech in order to figure out the answer. To be ideal, the question should be short and simple so that they can understand it well.

Quote a Relevant Research Study

Trust me when I tell you that you never know exactly who listen to you when you speak on the stage. But, one thing that you should know is that most, if not all, of them do not want to listen to you especially if you have no credentials. So, to attract their attention, you should learn to borrow some experts' knowledge to help you. Supposed your speech were about cancer, you would have to quote a research study from a famous cancer physician to help you. The quote could be some kind of new discovery or shocking statistics. You should use it well to attract their attention to listen to you.

## Chapter 5: But I Don't Want To Be A Public Speaker

There is a huge value to you with having the public speaking skill set even if you don't want to have a public speaking career. Learning the art of public speaking can help you immensely at your job, family and social life.

Applying these principles can and will help you in your job. Let's take a look. Think about this, your boss comes to you in a panic and states; here I need you to present this presentation at 11am (it's now 10:30am). The boss hands you a thumb drive which contains the presentation, which is scheduled for an hour and says that he has been called out on an emergency. As the boss is leaving he states "I'm counting on you to land this deal!" This can and does happen a lot in the corporate market. So if this happens to you, what would you do?

Here is not what to do. **Don't say "I can't do this!" because if you have visions on moving up the corporate latter that statement just put a big blockade in your advancement path.** First your boss would not have asked you if he did not think you had the product knowledge required. Unfortunately most don't even think about your speaking skills as it is assumed you know how. That is a harsh but true statement.

**Tips and Tricks**

So let's work with the above scenario. You have 30 minutes. Take 20 minutes to become familiar with the presentation. That's all that is required in this case. Take the time to review the presentation and make a few notes on some index cards, or something small on the important parts of the presentation. This should take only a few minutes. Now go through the presentation slide by slide to quickly determine how you will present the information. The last 10 minutes is for final preprep. Go to the meeting place and setup for the presentation. Make sure the projector is working and you have a remote to advance the slides during the presentation. Run through the slides again on the screen. This serves two purposes, 1. It allows you to assure yourself the presentation and the equipment are ready for the presentation and; 2. You get one more opportunity to see the presentation before you present it. As a result of this activity you have exposed yourself to this presentation three times.

Now the presentation; People start filing into the Conference Room, your mouth gets dry, your knees start shaking and your

stomach starts to turn. As my great Australian Office Assistant always tells me, "No Worries Mate". You go up and greet each and every attendee even if you know them. **DO NOT tell them you are standing in for anybody! You must come to the realization that this is now your presentation, not your bosses.** Your adrenalin should be flowing by now, right? So it is now time to get started. The introduction is next. Be careful not to say this presentation was just given to you at the last minute or something like that. You may think this might be a good way in your mind to relieve some of the pressure but you could not be more mistaken. If this type statement is used as an opening statement several things can happen. Let's take a look at them.
1. Your attendees could very well think that they were not important enough to have an assigned person for this presentation. Granted there was a person assigned but they do not want to hear it

was handed off at the last minute regardless of the reason.

2. Your attendees must feel that their value is very important for this meeting. If they think a stand in was brought in it could very well hurt the results you are trying to achieve.

Now, how do you present this information from this presentation being that you are unfamiliar with it where your audience does not know? **Remember one thing. They don't know what you don't know.** This is very important you as a presenter have control, or should have control of the conference room and your audience. You see there's no rule that you have to stand and face your audience with the screen behind you. With that in mind, there's nothing wrong with moving around. A good practice here is to move away from the screen and use it in your delivery as a tool. You may be asking yourself, what does that mean? Think about this, if you are standing behind your audience and

your
presentation is shown at the front of the room you can use it as an emphasis of your oral presentation. This is what I mean, let's say one of the bullet points on your presentation states, "I would like everyone to pay particular attention to this bullet point. The return on investment will be less than five years". Now consider that you read this write off the presentation, but because you added the statement "I would like everyone to pay particular attention to this bullet point." Allowed you to read this specific part of the presentation and your audience didn't know that. Is that cool or what?

This form of presenting works to exceptionally well when you haven't had the time to prepare adequately.

**Social                                    Environment**

Let's setup another scenario. Say you are invited to a dinner party. You ask who is going to be there, the dress and so on. You are told this is a business casual gathering of customers and executives from your company. You have two choices here 1. You can decline. This is really not a good idea if you have visions of moving up in the company. 2. You can accept.

So let's say you took option two. What do you need to know here? The general rule of thumb is understand the information explained in the Chapter 5 Pre Preparation. You must know your audience. There is no difference between knowing your audience at a speaking venue than there is at a business social event. Take the time to ask the organizer of this social event to advise you of the attendees. Unless you are a "wall flower" you will be talking with these people. There is also a chance you could be called upon to speak. **Don't assume this is just a dinner party as there is always a hidden agenda.** Get as much information from the organizer as you can.

As far as the business casual thing all I can say is, remember you are a walking billboard. Your presentation of yourself is important. Watch your consumption of alcohol. I know what a bummer right? But at one of these type events it's critical.

When it comes to public speaking I advise all of my clients that there is no difference to talking to one person than there is talking to 100.

So as you can see there is value to perfecting your communication skills even if you don't want to become a public speaker. You can apply the tools explained in this book to your everyday communication.

## Chapter 6: Collecting Nuggets Of Confidence

It's those little nuggets of confidence that help us grow as a speaker. You may be the speaker starting out who becomes frozen from fright or the one who paces like Liz in the previous chapter. What can you do to help build your confidence?

Let's look at four ways to do just that.

How you get confidence comes from doing something successfully.

First, you have to have confidence to speak in front of people, not ego or arrogance, CONFIDENCE. How do you get that???? How you get confidence comes from doing something successfully. Wouldn't you agree? Realizing that something worked because you finally did it right no matter how small it is. Every time you accomplish a goal, do something better, try something new, even with a little success, you are collecting nuggets of confidence. It may be hearing someone say, "Wow you did a great job, you've made me think in a whole new way." Or maybe they told you, "You finally stopped holding your hands in front of you."

These are the little nuggets of confidence you need to collect and it's important to have these to connect the pieces of the stage you are building in yourself. It's those little nuggets that help your confidence grow and make your stage stronger. Think of the nuggets as connectors that stop your stage from wiggling or swaying. They give you the confidence that you are building a solid foundation.

Take those simple nuggets, write them down on a page in your computer, notepad or phone and date them. Then six months or a year from now look at how your stage has strengthened. Collect and connect nuggets of confidence.

Don't let that fear of making mistakes stop you from forging ahead...

Second, it's no secret we all make mistakes. Don't let that fear of making mistakes stop you from forging ahead and continually learning and growing. If you give into that fear, you'll lose any ounce of confidence you've gained. You may make the same mistake two, three, four times ... but if you are aware of it and keep working on correcting it, that fifth time you'll do it right and it sure will feel good. Collect that nugget of confidence.

A mistake I made time after time after time when I started speaking was re-learning to hold for laughs. Now, I learned that as an actress ... but it got lost in my lack of continually working at my craft (there's a lesson right there). I didn't make that mistake once, I made it several times before I let my audience have the time to react and laugh. It's not about the mistake, it's about finally doing it right. Recognize what you did to make it work and be able to repeat that time and time again.

Third, when I was in undergraduate school in theatre I was like a sponge. Though my nervousness no longer showed as much on the outside it came out in another way, doubt filled with anxiety. Just another form of fear from lack of confidence.

"Take all that WASTEFUL nervous energy you have and use it on stage as positive energy for your audience."

It was one of my acting professors who told me one of the most important things I have ever learned. "Take all that WASTEFUL nervous energy you have and use it on stage as positive energy for your audience."

When I began to change my energy focus, things did begin to change for me. All that energy we waste on nervousness can be used as energy on the speaking platform to keep our audience engaged.

After all, who is nervousness about? It makes us focus on ourselves, when it should be used in a positive way for our audience. When we focus on ourselves we are giving our audience an empty message. I have never forgotten that lesson, so when you begin to get anxious before speaking simply say to yourself, "Positive energy for my audience. Positive energy for my audience."

Fourth, I'd like to share with you a simple exercise you can do that has helped me. On December 31, 2012, I sat in my living room asking myself, "What is the one thing I need to do in the new year to get where I need to be as a speaker, presenter, coach?" It was a kind of a New Year's Resolution for me. The first thing that came to my mind were the words "BE BOLD." I wrote those two words down in bold print on a little rubber duckie and left it on my side table next to my favorite chair, ensuring that I would see those words every morning.

So when I was asked to do something, even if it was out of my comfort zone, I would see those words flashing in my head "BE BOLD." I began taking bolder steps to improve and grow as a speaker. The words "BE BOLD" seemed to push me to a new level of confidence. They became my power words that year.

You can do this, too. Think about what it is that you want to accomplish in the coming year. Challenge yourself. What word or words are going to help push you to a new level of confidence?

Don't over think this ... just write down the first one or two words that come to your mind.

Take a moment now in a quiet place. Ask yourself this question, "What word or words are going to help push me to a new level of confidence?" Post those words in places you will see them every day. It doesn't have to be on a little rubber duckie. Most importantly, post that word or words in your mind. That's a nugget you can take anywhere with you.

Lastly, before I take on anything, if it's a private coaching session, doing volunteer work, or giving a speech to a group, I tell myself out loud, "I am great at this! This is my gift, I am going to rock today." Positive self-talk gives you confidence in the face of fear. What are you going to say to yourself?

Again, take a moment and write down no more than three short sentences. Make them short and to the point so they are easy to remember. Don't try to make it PERFECT ... you'll refine them over time. Just like I came up with my saying, you'll find yours.

In summary:

Collect nuggets of confidence even in the smallest of achievements—those nuggets will keep your wood planks together.

Think "Positive Energy for my audience."

Find your power words.
Write down and memorize your positive self-talk sentences.

## Chapter 7: How Creative Visualization Works

In a nutshell, creative visualization operates under the concept that whatever it is that you believe in will actually happen.

How exactly does that work? This seems like a fair question. Is there a scientific or logical explanation for creative visualization? How exactly can good and positive thoughts result into good and positive outcomes?

If creative visualization sounds too good to be true to you, that's probably because you are not yet aware of exactly how much focus and energy it takes to successfully execute creative visualization techniques. However, there really are ways by which creative visualization can be explained, in terms of how it works.

Here are some guidelines that help explain the workings behind the creative visualization process:

1) **Creative visualization works by providing clarity** . A lot of people are stuck in a rut due to confusion. They don't know what they're doing or what they actually want to do. They don't know who they're working with or dealing with. They don't know about they're timelines. Even when they know how to do things, they don't know the purpose why they do them — there's no answer to the big question, "**Why?**" There are people so busy engaging themselves in activities that they don't have the time to really think and pay attention. Creative visualization resolves all these problems because it can only be done when you have clarity, that is, when you have a clear and specific idea as to what it is that you want and how you can get it. This means that creative visualization forces you to "plan" as you imagine your scenario, and with that plan

in place, you are already as if fifty percent done with what you have to do.

2) **It also works by improving a person's capacity to focus** . Creative visualization would not make you a believer in multitasking. Instead, it will encourage you to focus all your efforts until you achieve your goals one by one. This makes it easy for you to eliminate distractions and be motivated to finish one task or one goal at a time as you maintain a positive and strong mental attitude that is ready to take on various challenges which you may end up using to your advantage.

3) **It activates a person's passion and motivation.** Creative visualization works by using a person's ability to perform with consistency. This is only possible when a person gets to activate his sense of passion. Passion is a greater degree of commitment. It's passion that separates people of mediocrity from people of achievement. It is what fuels perseverance and the capacity to succeed – the very

ingredients that creative visualization techniques imbibe in a person.

4) **It secures possibilities.** Creative visualization works because it dispels fears, reservations and uncertainties. Instead it focuses on prospects, chances and opportunities. By securing possibilities and ensuring in your mind that you can achieve what you plan to do, it enables you to take risks that you might otherwise not take because of fear of failure. By making you more certain of yourself, creative visualization, in effect, gives you more courage and confidence.

5) **Creative visualization works because similarities form a stronger bond of attraction.** Some people say that "opposites attract" while others say that "birds of the same feather flock together." Have you ever wondered which of these sayings are truer? In reality, similarities form a stronger bond than differences, especially when it comes to people and relationships. Creative visualization works

because it draws you near to people whose thoughts and actions are of the same caliber as the ones that you have. Notice how successful people surround themselves with like-minded individuals who are similar to them – people who collectively value perfection, excellence, diligence and success. Creative visualization works in pretty much the same way, but it trains to you have a winner's mindset right from the very beginning.

6) **Creative visualization goes through steps or stages.** What makes creative visualization techniques quite effective is that it starts by making you familiar with small accomplishments or what you may call "small steps," and then it leads you to achieving big accomplishments or taking big leaps later on. This gradual increase in experiencing various levels of success will build your confidence and enable you to understand how creative visualization can take you further.

## Chapter 8: Four Questions About Leadership

I hear four questions asked about leadership usually. This chappter gives a short answer to everyone of these essential questions.
Why Does Leadership Matter?
Parents universally hope that their children develop leadership qualities. They know that leaders are people who are efficient in what they do, are respected by others, and typically rewarded for those skills in a number of ways. It is in these formative years that, through our parents,

we first see leadership as desirable and essential.

As young people we look up to people around us that motivate and listen to us; people that seem like "real-life" heroes. We consider these people leaders. As we grow we begin to relate leaders to their jobs - ministers, teachers, police officers. And later Mayors, Presidents, and CEO's.

As adults all of these thoughts and experiences define why we think leaders have desirable traits and play roles we admire (and why we desire these things for our children).

All of these experiences and thoughts help us define why leadership matters - it matters since leaders make a difference and could shape the future. It matters since leaders are valued and valuable. In everyone's mind leadership, particularly when it is good, matters.

What's a Leader?

A leader is a person who sees something

that must be done, knows that they could help make it happen, and gets began.
A leader sees opportunity and captures it. A leader sees a future that could be different and greater, and assists others see that picture too.
A leader knows they can't do it alone.
A leader is a coach.
A leader is an encourager.
A leader views change as their ally.
A leader is willing to take risks today for something greater tomorrow.
A leader is a learner.
A leader is a communicator.
A leader is a coordinator.
A leader is a listener.
A leader takes a long view - allowing their vision keep their daily steps on track.
A leader is passionate.
A leader motivates and inspires.
A leader values results.
A leader cares about more than results though; she cares about those who're following her lead.

A leader makes a difference in the lives of others.

A leader is all of these things and much more.

Are People Born Leaders?

Sure they are - I mean everybody is born, right?

You may say that riddle-like answer misses the point. You say the real answer is that quite a few people are really born to lead. And I would reply that your common statement implies that others aren't born to be leaders.

So let's examine that difference of opinion...

When individuals describe somebody as a "born leader" they typically mean that the person is motivating, a good communicator and charismatic. In fact it is true; many people are blessed at birth with more natural capacity in these ways. But leaders could be terrific with various innate characteristics as well. And there is no single tiny skill set that defines the perfect leader or guarantees success.

Everybody is born with a unique set of natural capabilities. And most of us could develop skills and styles to complement those natural capabilities.

Who is a Leader?

This question on the surface is the easiest question I've asked so far. After all, I've already given a number of examples. People in specified roles are leaders, whether they've studied for the role, like a physician, lawyer, teacher or minister... got elected to the role, like a county councilman, mayor, Senator or President... or worked up the through the organization like a supervisor, manager, Vice President or CEO.

You could ask most anybody the question "Who is a leader?" and those are the types of answers they will give you. They are right, obviously. But they are only partially right.

Leaders aren't leaders simply because of a

job title. Leaders are leaders since they lead. Which takes me back to my previous question - "Are people born leaders?" Yes they are. But it isn't just a few that have been hand picked by our Creator or random genetics. Most of us have been picked - genetics has selected us all. We were all born to lead, in our own way. We might not be the Chairman of the Board. We might not be the person on the stage.

We might not lead with oratory or flair. We might lead by compassion. We might lead by example. We all could lead. We all have the capability to be remarkable leaders. Leadership isn't about position. Leadership isn't about power. Leadership is about potential - your potential.

You are a leader. Claim and believe this to

be true, for it is. Stake your claim and make a difference in the world around you.

Your opportunities for leadership are unlimited. The rewards are boundless. My answers to four questions lead to a question for you...
Where will you lead?

## Chapter 9: To Control Fear You Need To Understand Fear

Everybody knows fear is a mental construct do they not? I mean you know this is true, am I right?

It is all in your head as they say.

You have probably heard the old saw about FEAR being, "**F**alse **E**vidence **A**ppearing **R**eal."

It is catchy, and it is memorable but is it right?

Here is the thing to ask yourself. If it is all in your head, why do you feel so bad physically when you are scared?

When the fear of public speaking or presenting grips you, you know all about it because your body reacts in certain predictable ways; often uncomfortable and sometimes even embarrassing ways. It is the same for high stakes selling or negotiating situations or difficult conversations with a friend or family member. It is the same for any stressful communication activity. Your body lets you know you are scared.

This is because there is a real link between what and how you think and how you feel and behave physically. The reverse is also true; how you feel can readily influence how you think and it can influence the quality of your thinking.

Here is a relatively simplistic view of the overall mental and physiological processes which we call fear. It might well help you to know this basic sequence of events is happening the next time you experience fear because you can learn to break the cycle.

One thing I would like to stress here before we go any further is this; it is sensible to be scared. Fear is generally regarded as being a beneficial emotional reaction for you to have. Without it you simply would not live too long. Having realistic fears about snakes, heights and fast-moving traffic will keep you alive longer than say, picking up sidewinders, walking carelessly along cliff edges and crossing the street without looking left and right. Obvious, yes?

You may well have heard of the "fight or flight" response which we all have. We developed this as a species to enable us to react quickly and fully automatically to strange developing situations which may have been hazardous to our health as early humans. Sabre-toothed tigers, mammoths, huge bears, hostile tribes, etc... For example, "Is that rustling in the bushes a threat?" If our ancestors had paused to stop and think it might have been too late and we would not be here today. The fact that we are here suggest our ancestors chose to run first and ask questions later. Many of the historical threats are not valid now, but there are still many valid threats out there. We still have the autonomous and automatic response of fear and fight or flight. To be more precise it is fight, flight, faint or freeze.

Interestingly, the physiological response to fear is essentially the same as for any other emotion. You detect the developing situation at an automatic yet unidentified low level of bodily arousal and then seek a logical cause to assign to it. A noise in the dark – fear. An attractive potential partner – lust. Adrenaline, cortisol and other potent chemicals begin to flood your body just the same.

These chemicals trigger many bodily responses including a racing heart, fast breathing, energised muscles and many others. One of the bodily responses is the reduced capacity of your neocortex and other analytical/emotional areas of the brain. This leaves you with the effective mental capacity of let us say a well-educated Rhesus monkey. This is not much help in a tight spot, but it does go a long way to explaining road rage and other modern tantrum based behaviours.

The following is an incredibly simple description of the mental activity in a stressful situation. It is provided as a model only. In any stressful or frightening situation your brain utilises two internal routes to process and deal with it – one extremely fast and one a little bit slower. A part of your brain called the thalamus initiates both. The fast route is a fully automatic "just in case there's a problem I'll shoot first and ask questions later" mode where your raw information gathering thalamus talks directly to another part of your brain called the amygdala and says the equivalent of "Hey, this situation is unusual - am I supposed to be scared or something?" Your amygdala checks its repository of fear memories and associated strong emotional reactions then, if it decides the raw information from the thalamus is indeed a good enough match with one of them, it kicks in the adrenal-cortical system and via another part of your brain called the hypothalamus.

Forget all the technical phrases, this is the bit where your bowels can get a bit unreliable, if you know what I mean.

If not quickly stopped this goes on to produces the full flight or fight response and associated behaviour; you either get aggressive or you run away. As mentioned, there are in fact two more options available to your automatic system and they are faint or freeze; neither of which are much use.

The brain areas we are talking about here reside in a biologically much older region of your brain which is known as your limbic brain.

The slower route utilises two biologically and evolutionarily younger brain areas called the sensory cortex and the hippocampus (and quite a few more which have been left out here for reasons of simplicity) to analyse and question the same incoming data arriving from your thalamus along with any other relevant and/or freshly available information to decide whether the perceived threat is real or not. If not considered real, it will send a "stand down" message back to the amygdala which then switches off the hypothalamus response – in other words you feel a few moments of panic then you calm down.

If the sensory cortex and hippocampus team also decided the perceived threat is real after all then the hypothalamus can carry on and, depending on the situation, may just save your life. It is what the whole automatic system is for after all.

The above information is interesting enough but perhaps far more interesting to you, in your situation as a nervous speaker, is developing an understanding about the body reacting the same way whether the fear is real or imagined. Seriously, our minds can really struggle to determine the difference between real events and remembered events. The brain uses the exact same mental and neuronal circuitry to process both versions. Therefore, unless you learn and practice rationalising and controlling the signals your brain generates when you are thinking about public speaking the amygdala response can easily be hijacked by these internal signals and you will create your classic stage fright or freezing fear of public speaking just by thinking about it.

I am sure you will agree, there are enough technical things to worry about when preparing to speak without shredding your nerves and piling on the stress by allowing your own imagination to trigger a mental and bodily fear response.

Here is the good news. Knowing all this now means you can control the situation with effort and practice, and thus reducing the imaginary effects, until the fear of public speaking no longer holds you in its thrall.

Going back to our original question about FEAR being "False Evidence Appearing Real," for our purposes I recommend thinking more along the lines of Speaking fear being self-generated evidence appearing real. You can reduce the self-generated false evidence to reduce the fear.

What follows in the first half of this guide is all designed to help you understand, rationalise and therefore work to reduce the unknowns when speaking in public which cause you to worry most. Believe in the tools and techniques and practice the various methods to identify and deal with your nerves and you will improve your control, reduce your nerves and be a better speaker.

Ultimately you will learn to fully embrace your speaking nerves and you will welcome them like an old friend.

Chapter action points

Think back to the last time you were required to speak in public. Only you will know the answers to these questions so be as honest as possible. If you were scared you were scared, you must acknowledge and accept things before you can move on. When you answer the questions remember to be kind to yourself, you did not know how not to be scared at that point in time.

How did you feel mentally and physically when you were first asked or told to speak?

If you have spoken in public before, think back to the time a week or so ahead of the event and ask yourself the same question.

Now think back to how it felt just before the speaking event. Were you excited, nervous or out and out terrified?

Can you use the information in the "Understanding Fear" chapter to get a better picture of what happened automatically in your body during these distinct phases of the fear process?

What could you potentially do differently next time to control your reactions and take on a more useful mental and physiological state?

Why not have a chat with some more experienced speakers and try to get a feel for their answers to the above questions. You may well find that speaking nerves are more common than you think. They can overcome them and so can you.

## Chapter 10: General Tips For Public Speaking

This chapter is dedicated to give you a couple of tips to help get you started in public speaking. Although this book will help you come up with great speeches in a step-by-step manner, this section gives you general guidelines that great public speakers observe.

Assess yourself. Identify your strengths, enhance them, and flaunt them. For instance, if you are a good storyteller, then make sure that your speech contains good relevant stories that your audience can relate to.If you have fresh and good humor, spice up your message with a couple of jokes which people can generally relate to.

Listen to good speakers.

You need to experience being a member of the audience in order to identify what makes a good speaker. Try to have a "model person" who you can emulate. Evaluate this person, identify his strengths and weaknesses, and do the best you can to even become better.

Prepare.

**Know your topic.** You should be able to provide information–something new–something that your audience can use. If they know as much about a topic as you do, then you have nothing new to offer and you will be wasting their time.

**Analyze your audience.** Knowing your audiences' demographics will help you plan your speech in a much better way. More than anything, you have to get a general idea on what your audiences expect for the speaking engagement.

**Visualize the event.** Before the actual event, visit the venue where you will be holding your speech. Get a feel of the stage and the number of audiences that you have. This can give you an idea on how you can best present yourself.

Constantly improve your communication skills.

Public speaking is after all, a form of communication. Always practice your verbal communication skills—the construction of your sentences, the flow of your messages, the organization of your thoughts, your pronunciation, and your overall delivery of a message.

Observe good posture.

Good posture projects an aura of confidence, credibility, and authority.

Speak clearly, confidently, and audibly.

You don't want to sound like you're eating your own words, so speak as clearly as possible. Avoid speaking too fast as your audience may also fail to understand you. Practice recording your speeches and listen to them so you can evaluate your performance.

Use short sentences.

Why use short sentences over long ones? This is to make things simple both for you and for your audience. Shorter sentences tend to be more powerful and easier to understand. They are also easier to say and remember. By using short sentences, you minimize the possibility of getting lost in your own thoughts.

Use a variety of techniques to maintain your audiences' attention.

Although your speech's introduction should especially be catchy, you need to exert some effort on making your speech more exciting, and here, the key is variety. Ask questions, tell stories, cite examples, anecdotes, quotations, historical characters, current events–all things new, relevant, and familiar–use them to captivate your audience.

Look your best.

When it comes to attire, the rule of thumb is to dress better than your audience does. The way you look will build your audience's first impression of you. Being pleased with how you look will also boost your confidence.

Practice delivering different types of speeches.

There are speeches which you read, speeches that you memorize, and speeches that you deliver extemporaneously. Be able to deliver all types and familiarize yourself with different kinds of speeches, too:

**Informative** – introducing new topics, speeches similar to professors' short lectures

**Demonstrative** – how-to speeches

**Persuasive** – convincing people to **do** something

**Entertaining speeches** – after-dinner speeches, speeches for special occasions

Respond to audience feedback.

In order to be an effective communicator, you need to understand your audience, and be flexible enough to respond to their needs. For instance, if you see raised eyebrows in your audiences, what does it mean? They may be surprised with what you just said, so you need to respond by providing them more information/explanation. Meanwhile, if your audience isn't making eye contact, then it shows that they are uninterested and you need to get their attention.

Personalize your speech.

What makes your speech unique? You. You are your most valuable asset. Own your speech. Talk about your own stories, your own experiences, your own views, your own research, and your own beliefs. By talking about your "own," you will see that your anxiety will decrease. After all, how can you go wrong when you're talking about yourself?

## Chapter 11: Narrowing Down Your Subject

Most of the time, you will know your subject- it will not be something you have a choice about. You will know it because it will relate to something you are selling or a point you are attempting to get across. So subject matter is not always a choice in many situations.

But for those of us who do choose our subject, we must choose carefully. If we choose too broad of a subject we will lose the audience with too much information, and we will not do the subject justice. If we choose too narrow of a subject, we will not have enough information and will repeat the same things over and again. Either way, we will bore our audience and will not be successful in conveying our message. We must learn over time to choose our subject wisely and to know just how much time to spend on that subject. This is a delicate thing which requires the accumulation of knowledge. Do the research, get the information, and then weed out things that are not necessary. Many times I will have many pages of information that I must go through to reduce the amount of information I will be sharing. I have a small time slot to get the information across. The attention span of the average American is short at best. When you are watching TV, you will notice that every 6 or 10 minutes there are commercial breaks. Does that tell you anything? Every few minutes we need to shift gears- interject into our speech something to give their brains a break. This gear shifting could be a funny story, a visual aid, or just a funny remark. This is like a commercial- it is off the subject or it compliments the subject, but it is a light moment that will allow your listener to hold on a few more minutes and listen intently.

No matter how important your subject matter may be, this fact remains: your audience will not be able to stay tuned to you for long periods of time without their mind wandering and their ears going to sleep. So now you know the importance of selecting your subject carefully, researching it thoroughly and select only the most important information to persuade your audience. If you are not willing to do the work, you will not enjoy the benefits of a great speech. **A wise professor once said, "You can no more speak about something you don't know than you can come back from somewhere you have never been."**

## Chapter 12: Becoming Larger Than Life

To say that there is no ego in a person who does public speaking regularly or for a living would be clearly a false statement. But for those of us who only speak from time to time, when you see a speaker who can walk out in a room of 30 people or a auditorium of 3000 and literally "own the room", it really is an amazing transformation. To imagine how you could ever be that much larger than life is mind boggling.

But in a lot of ways, when you step out to talk to a group of people, you do become larger than life. That is because you are doing the impossible. You are having a conversation with dozens of people all at once. Now, whether you feel like you are having that conversation or not isn't important. If your talk is not interactive, you may not know the dialog is happening. But in the minds of every single individual in that hall, they are interacting with you.

What you are saying is getting down inside of them and they are reacting to it. But even more than what you are saying, how you are saying it is having an even bigger impact.

So are there things you can do to "become" larger than life? Well there are some ways of behaving in front of a crowd that differ from daily life. We do have to accept that you will develop a 'stage persona" that is different from your daily personality when you speak to a group. Does that make you a phony? No. Both of those personalities are you. It is just a different you when you relate to a group than to people one on one and it seems strange because that form of you only comes out on stage. But it isn't a Dr. Jekyll, Mr. Hyde thing. Just as you speak to a child differently than you speak to an adult, you will develop a way to talking to a group that differs from speaking to an individual.

Part of becoming larger than life is learning to what they call "own the room". This sound egotistic and strange but it really does work when you are about to speak. Owning the room simply means that when you step out in front of that crowd, they are no longer some random group of people, they are YOUR people. They are there to listen to you and what you say is of value to them. If you had any ego problems before you stepped out in front of that audience, check that ego problem at the door.

You must assume that you are adored when you speak to a group of people. This doesn't mean you strut about like God's gift to the world. But it does mean that you recognize that your value to this group is as a speaker and that your services are wanted and needed here. In fact, the only way you will be an effective public speaker is if you own the room. Treat that room like it was your home and these people came here just because being with you is just that great. If you step out there with that attitude, the audience will buy into your attitude and they will give you the room and be glad you took it over.

It can be a bit strange if you watch yourself become larger than life. But you can be humble about it and just recognize it is part of the craft of becoming a great public speaker. And if being good at this art you are gifted to give to the world means owning rooms and becoming bigger for an hour or so, well then why deny the world that experience? Enjoy it and let others enjoy it too.

## Organizing Your Professional Speaking Presentation

You may have just been asked to make a presentation by your boss or maybe, you're starting on a new professional speaking career. Whatever the case may be, starting your presentation means you'll have a ton of details to organize into a relatable format for your audience. Here are some tips on how to do just that.

One of the most difficult aspects of making your presentation is getting started. You may be feeling overwhelmed even if you've been working with your materials for years. Maybe you're looking for a way to simplify your research process. In any case, the first step is to jump in there and get started.

1. Research your material. Collect and read as much information as possible. Make some notes and also look at the validity of the information you are collecting. Is the information outdated? Is it relevant to the actual subject you are going to talk about? Start taking notes and highlighting potentially key points of your presentation.

2. Once you feel you've gathered enough information to present, review your notes and select the information you are going to present. Look for key ideas that support the purpose of your talk. Decide how deep you will go when presenting your information? Consider your audience.

What do they need to know to take action on your subject? How much detail do they actually need? Consider also, the length of the time you'll have for your presentation.

3. Organize your key ideas into an outline form. Start with the key points you will make and add two to three supporting elements to it. When you speak, you will be leading your audience from point A to point B. You're taking them somewhere even if it's only in their minds. Does your outline show a path to take? Is it relevant? Adjust your key points until you do lead your audience to where you want them to go.

4. Decide how you will present your organized information in your presentation. What visual aids can you use to strengthen your points? Is there data or research that you can bring into your presentation? How can you vary the delivery of your message? Your

presentation will be more interesting if you do more than just talk. People can easily tune out of your message especially if it's during a meal or immediately following one.

5. Organize your presentation outline to incorporate your visuals and method of delivery in your presentation. Review what it looks like on paper. Your outline is like your map for success. Is your map clearly defining the information you want to say? Are there any weak points were the information is not as strong as you'd like it to be? If it's not, revise and review and keep doing this until you get your map the way you want it to be.

Organizing the material for your presentation is a process. As you take your audience from lack of knowledge to having knowledge, your background work is to create an outline map of your journey. This map is the key to your success and the only way to be successful is to have a plan of action. Start today in creating your map of success!

## How To Write A Speech

You cannot excel at public speaking without a good speech. If you are asked to give a speech or its required for work or school, you know that when you stand up there to give that presentation, you are going to have to have a well organized outline and content to get through it and impress those listening. Sometimes the fear of an upcoming speaking engagement comes from that writers block that happens when you have to write a good speech.

Writing a speech is not exactly like writing a term paper or a report. The reason is simple. What you actually "write" is not intended to be read. It will be heard. You don't have to worry about good spelling or the other conventions of writing a paper because it might never see the light of day. If you are new to writing speeches, it might be best to write it out like a paper so you can hear it being said in your head.

But many times experienced speakers write a speech in the form of an outline based on a defined structure and then they hang the detail off of the structure. The detail is the content and the substance of the speech which makes up why your speech has value. It can include quotations, facts, historical references, scientific statistics, whatever you need to support the theme of your speech.

Now how you organize your speech may be determined by what kind of speech it is. And what kind of speech it is can be defined by what you hope to achieve. So a speech might be designed to convince, to sell, to entertain or to inform. Many times a speech can be a combination of these forms. But you should define what your expected outcome so you know if you have achieved your goal by the time the composition of the speech is done. Having that overriding goal well in mind helps in how you organize your speech.

The skeleton of a good speech is similar to a paper. But lay out each section and allocate your time accordingly even before you write the speech. The components are the introduction, the opener, the personal introduction, the statement of the "problem", three to five points of the body of the speech, the summary and the closer or the call for action again depending on the purpose of the speech.

For the opener, its good to use something that brings the audience to you. Its good to greet them warmly and seek a greeting in response. Some anecdote about the hall or the weather even can get the talk off on the right foot. Then go into your personal information but making sure what you tell relates to why you are the one here giving this talk. Keep every aspect of the presentation relevant to the central theme.

The problem statement can be phrased as a question. A good speech is like a good story because you must create a problem and then solve it. If you are going to discuss tricks for using Microsoft PowerPoint, start out talking about problems using the software with illustrations about catastrophes that have been caused by that lack of understanding. As much as possible keep the problem relevant your listeners. Then move directly from there to presenting the body of your work in an organized way. Make sure you have three to five solid points. Tell them what they are, tell them the points and then tell them what you just said. That cements your presentation in their minds.

The conclusion is often a summary of what was just said. Its good to close with humor as well. But you may also use the final summary of your talk for any call to action you may have in mind for this audience. If they enjoyed your speech, they want to know what you want them to do, even if they are not going to go do that. It just gives a nice ending to the discussion. Thank them for their time and close. But stick around because if it was a good talk, you will have questions or people who will want to talk to you about things they thought about afterward. And if that happens, you know for certain then that you did a good job.

## Chapter 13: The Benefits Of Public Speaking

"Management is about persuad ing people to do things they do not want to do, while leadership is about inspiring people to do things they never thought they could (Steve Jobs)

"Communication is blood of life blood of organization" (Peter Drucker). The same is true when it comes to our social life. Influence happens through communication. Most of our daily energy goes into influencing other whether it is through our physical beauty, grooming, nice clothes, fancy cars, ideas and expressions. All these are aimed at influencing others. However, communication is the best source of influencing others. A public speaker is always treated at a higher pedestal.

Public speaking is the apex of Communication skills. When you have mastered the art of effective communication at the public arena, you can reap unimaginable benefits in professional and personal life. A person with effective communications skill has unlimited opportunities. Let's see some of them:

Benefits of public speaking

Public speaking is the act of courage and leads to the road to limelight and leadership Public speaking is also risking self in front of the audience, because neither the audience reaction is predictable nor your performance on the stage. Even the best speaker may fumble. However, it is worth taking the baton of public speaking because of multiple benefits it brings. Some of them are as under:

1. Developing courage

Public speaking is the number one fear and once you take the effort to overcome or master that fear, it opens you up tremendously. It takes lot of courage to stand up on the stage and talk to a bunch of people even to a small gathering of known office colleagues or relatives. However, every time you face your fear on the stage, it makes you the more courageous person in the process. It makes you highly confident in the personal and social arena. One can overcome the fear of public speaking with preparation and practice.

2. Boost self-esteem

Let's face it, a person who can't face the audience, howsoever, accomplished he might be, lacks in self-esteem. He doesn't feel measured up vis-à-vis the audience even though the audience may be less qualified and less fortunate. When your self-esteem is low, you social confidence is low. Can a person ever be a leader, who cannot address the audience and lacks in confidence? The answer is NO. Stantley Coopersmith in his book, "The Antecedents of SelfEsteem" has defined self-esteem:

"By self-esteem, we refer to the evaluation which the individual makes and customarily maintains with regards to himself. It expresses an attitude of approval or disapproval, and indicates the extent to which the individual believes in himself to be capable, significant, successful, and worthy."

In short, self-esteem is a personal judgment of worthiness that is expressed in the attitudes the individual holds toward himself. The self-esteem is about valuing self and also being sensible to others. When you feel good and comfortable about yourself, your selfesteem is high. Selfesteem is confidence in one's thought or decision-making and courage to take on the challenges of life without undue fear. It is standing on one's own feet and being authentic self on the one hand and constantly striving to raise the bar. We spend most of our life getting approvals of the others. Whether you believe it ornot.

Probably, that's why we are very conscious about our public image. Therefore, when we excel on the stage, it zooms our self-esteem to another level.

Confident people have a greater chance of becoming a better public speaker. Simply because they are more comfortable with themselves and have the courage to present themselves as they are in public. Most importantly they are able to sway the audience to their viewpoint.

See the paradox, the more successful and famous you become, the more conscious you become towards the public image. Since the sunk cost is high, the fear of falling or stumbling before the audience is heightened. Hence, if you are bad or average in your public speaking, your tendency to overcome it drastically diminishes with your progress. However, like for the King George VI, it remains a nightmare, not to be able to speak in public eloquently and confidently. "To thine own self-be true. And it must follow, as the night the day, Thou canst not then be false to any man" (Shakespeare). It is very important to dig down and ask whether you are truly comfortable with yourself. Because when you be comfortable with yourself, you will be comfortable with others as well.

Public speaking is scary and it really is but it is worth taking that fear directly. Because it is also one of the most assured ways of boosting self-esteem. It is not what you get at the end but what you become in the process. Once you master the fear, the stage would become one of the favorite places. The teachers, coaches, motivational trainer know the high that the public speaking gives. You can observe that public speakers have comparatively higher self-esteem than those who fear to speak in public.

I still remember the day, when I gave my first speech in front of my classmates in 11th standard. My class teacher allotted a Chapter each to all the students and asked us to read and speak about it for 5 to 10 minutes. I chose a Chapter titled, 'Gehu aur Gulab' ('Wheat and Rose'). I liked the topic, it was about the basic necessities of life (Food, shelter) and beauties of life (art, knowledge, love and other higher aspect of life). I prepared thoroughly and to my amazement, I delivered it very well. My class teacher and classmates were also surprised at my performance since I was very casual in studies and fun-loving person. They rated it as the best speech. It was one of the turning points of life when I realized my potential as a speaker and a person. I realized the immense satisfaction and self-esteem that the public speaking brings in. Since then I have moved towards the art of public speaking.

3. Expression begets satisfaction

Expression of one's thought and idea to a group of people gives lots of satisfaction. Humans are social animals and it is necessary instinct to express our view. It is observed that those who are not able to express their view clearly suffer from low esteem, stunted social personality and fearfulness. When we are able to express our views eloquently to the audience, it satisfies our urge of expression. It is one of the best avenues of self-expression at par with singing and dancing.

The ability and outlet to express oneself in the desired manner is one of the most satisfying experiences. We all want our ideas and feelings to find proper expression and acceptance. When you are good in public speaking, you can fulfill both of your desire of selfexpression and acceptance. If you strike the right chord with the audience, you can enjoy huge support and influence. To influence others is one of the most attractive things to have. Public speaking gives lots of satisfaction through the ability to express.

4. Leadership

The final edge at the top of the ladder is decided on the communication skill. As elucidated in the Introduction, how the novice king faced with a challenge of his own mannerism of addressing to his people due to his poor communication skill and fear. There is another classic example of Manmohan Singh, former Prime Minister of India, which proves that no amount of academic brilliance and knowledge can compensate for the lack of powerful public speaking skill and persona when it comes to leadership at the highest level. He was one of the most brilliant persons who has worked on all the key post in India viz, Planning Commission Chairman, Finance Minister (drafted the famous 1991 liberalization policy of India) and then Prime Minister for 10 years. However, his feeble leadership style was obvious when he led India for a decade as the Prime Minister. Leading such a high and important public position entails leading from the front. It required one to be vocal and expressive about the vision and mission of the nation. However, he was too docile and worked as a sincere and dedicated expert rather than a leader. No wonder he was called as Accidental Prime Minister of India.

In boxing, Mohammed Ali (great speaker in the ring as well as outside, a poet, a writer) is far more famous than any other boxer not just due to his excellent boxing but also for his aggressive press conferences and communication skill than any other boxer or other great athletes. In Cricket, more expressive players like Saurav Ganguly and M.S Dhoni were chosen captain over genius but introvert Sachin Tendulkar. The top is dominated by the one who can speak well, given the same amount of talent, knowledge or even with less of that.

In business, the powerful speakers and presenters like Steve Jobs, Warren Buffet, Elon Musk, Jack Welch, Mark Cuban, Grant Cordane, Jack Ma have ruled the business world and taken it to the next level.

Even in the field of religion and spirituality, the masters with powerful speaking capabilities like Osho, J. Krishnamurti, Jaggi Vasudev, Sri Sri Ravi Shankar and preachers like Joel Osteen, Joyce Meyers are considered as the forerunner in hogging the limelight and leading people towards their line of thinking.

5. Unlimited opportunities

The art of communication and negotiations skills had unlimited job opportunities. Sales being one of the industries which is the common denominator to all the industries, a good communication skill and the ability to influence the audience are powerful talent and are very crucial. Since all the industries and professions survive due to sales, there are unlimited growth opportunities. Besides, good communication and public speaking skill has a wide scope and all the management post requires it. Hence, there is no limit to income and growth.

6. Speaking is paying business

Communication driven business and profession is at all-time high. The new genre of call center companies, advertising agencies, personality development centers and public speaking institutes etc. are making a good amount of money. The rise of journalists, motivational speakers, life coaches, consultants, spiritual gurus proves the immense potential of earning well through public speaking capability.

Of late, successful celebrities like former US President Bill Clinton and his wife Hillary Clinton, former UK PM Tony Blair (highest grosser) and celebrity from non-speaking background sportsman like Roger Federer, Andre Agassi, Steffi Graff or writer like Robert Greene, Malcolm Gladwell or financial experts like Warren Buffet, Alan Greenspan, Ben Bernanke etc. are being paid handsome amount to speak to the business and management leaders.

7. Speaking ability adds to more success and admiration

The communication skills of Cricketers like Sunil Gavaskar, Ravi Shastri, Navjot Singh Sidhu or actors like Shahrukh, Shekhar Suman or political leaders like Bill Clinton, Tony Blair or sportsman like, Mohammed Ali brings a lot of admiration and accolades. Their speaking abilities have augmented their influence to a much larger horizon than their field of expertise.

8. Public speaking brings better opportunities and popularity

Public speaker hog the limelight and remain etched in our memories longer. It creates branding or PR advertisement for you. Familiarity begets love and support in a very subtle manner. The known face creates liking, which helps one for getting important assignments, faster promotions recognition in the office and even opportunities for important meetings and official foreign trips. The dictum, out of sight, out of mind holds true. Hence, public speaking keeps you alive in the memories of a larger audience, which brings more visibility to the speaker and helps in developing a large network. It also leads to many opportunities and windfall gain since senior and influential people might spot you as the right candidate for their business and project.

9. Necessary Skill

Communication is the essential for an organization. As a professional, you need to communicate externally to your customers, government officials, regulators and internally to your subordinates, peers, and seniors. Besides, making a presentation is a part of the corporate world, wherein you have to display your public speaking ability. Ability is to speak persuasively is a much sought after skill. The higher one goes up the ladder in the organization or stature, higher the need for the effective communication. A good speaking ability helps you establish a good reputation and often gives an edge over others with higher academic qualification.

Communication skill is a necessary skill in the business world.

10. Professional credibility

A professional with good public speaking ability brings credibility to himself and his organization. The way you speak while giving a presentation to your senior or customers or when you speak at conferences etc., it substantially adds to credibility. The launching of Apple I phone by Steve Jobs was a great marketing campaign, which brought lot of attention and curiosity among the customers. What people bought was not just the excellent product but trust and reputation of Steve Jobs and the company.

11. Networking

When you speak well, you will be instantly famous and be the cynosure of the audience. It results in an opportunity for making friends and building business contacts. This visibility as a speaker widens your networking. When people see you speaking on the dais, they see you with high self-esteem and prefer to connect with you vis-à-vis hundreds of unknown of people in the audience.

## 12. Good relationship

Expression of feelings is sine quo non for building and maintaining a healthy relationship. A person with good communication is better placed to interact with more people and with greater frequency, thereby making his relationship quotient stronger. Good public speaking is no guarantee for a good relationship. However, good speakers generally are better at relationship. As they can overcome the strained relationship with their communication skill by displaying enough confidence to their spouse, seniors or colleagues to believe them. People particularly women hate most the person who is closed and not open to open communication. Though people publically say they dislike flattering but personally they relish it and fall for it.

Good speakers also possess and develop a strong convincing ability.

13. Improve knowledge and thinking

Public speaking needs preparation. Natural public speaker is a chimera. When you write a speech, it makes you think critically and it expands your horizon when you study to collect materials to prepare it. Further, when you speak in front of an audience, you start thinking on feet. As you progress in your public speaking, you even add something to and modify your speech depending on the direct feedback and reaction of the audience. The process of writing and delivering a speech is a very powerful method to develop your critical thinking. Further, public speaking opens up you to questions and argument from the audience. In defending your views you also learn to argue, which keeps your 'thinking- hat' active.

14. Sharpen the art of persuasion

Every communication is an act of persuasion. However, when the magnitude increases to public speaking, you learn the art of persuading people at a greater degree. Persuading one person is easy rather than persuading a group of people. Bigger the group, bigger the challenge. Public speaking enables one to develop man management skill by enabling them to gauge the aspirations, expectations and the likely response of the audience. Further, it also develops the ability to handle objections, arguments, and opposition from the audience thereby making the art of persuasion more strong.

15. Better interpersonal Skill:

Public speaking makes us think not only about the topics but also about the audience. It gives us the confidence to share our messages and the skill to understand, to present our ideas and message in a sensitive and respectful manner. Public speaking skills also help us understand people better. It enables us to understand audiences' perspectives, needs, expectation, sensitive zone, bias, cultural and intellectual leaning etc. In the process of developing our public speaking skill, we also improve our interpersonal skill.

## Chapter 14: Courage And Confidence

Getting rid of fear
"You do not run away because you are afraid. You are afraid because you run away from you fear?
**Steven Spielberg, Hollywood film maker, with a ring of blockbusters declares.**"My greatest fear is speaking in public. Fear of insects takes second place. I remember during a conference I was giving to students of American law, completely forgetting how to speak English, my mother language: I started to think in French. It only lasted a minute or two, but it was terrifying."
Have you ever this kind of panic bred from fear? Have you ever had to express yourself in front of others, only to find out you have lost all your faculties? Or, are you just afraid of being placed in such situation one day?

Fear is the result of ignorance and uncertainty. One way of not being afraid of your fear is to become familiar with it and understand it.

Fear can assume a number of forms (apprehension, stage fright, anxiety, tension, and nervousness) is a preparation for action.

Research shows that the mechanism works as follows:

**1**. Announcement of an event

**2**. Association with previous events

**3**. Preparing body and mind for action

**4**. Images of what can happen

Where does fear enter into this process?

The emotion of fear begins at stage 2, the association with previous events. Most people try to work on 4. Their blood vessels are already transporting quantities of stress hormones. Their hearts are pumping like mad. They sweat, they are feverish or cold or both.

There are ways to control the effects of this fear known as stage fright. The most advanced method, such as positive thinking, suggests tackling at 3, creating reassuring and positive images of what can happen. This is partially effective but, it often creates an inner conflict. "It is only by destroying the roots of our fear that we can overcome."

There are number of ideas associated with stage frights, which are inherent in our way of thinking: "You can never get rid of stage fright."

"You cannot conquer stage fright, but you can control it."

Stage fright is necessary to perform well in public, but you don't have to suffer to succeed. We think of the price we have to pay to perform well. It's a little like the curse placed on Adam and Eve after their expulsion from the Garden of Eden.' You will bear in suffering.'

Giving a speech is like giving birth and just as there are methods to give birth without much pain, so are there methods that allow you to avoid the pain of stage fright.

To build courage and confidence:

**1**. Start with a strong and persistent desire.

**2**. Know your subject thoroughly.

**3**. Act confident. (Fake it till you make it)

**4**. Practice! Practice! Practice!

Things to remember:

Sources of Speaking Anxiety Communication researchers have identified three types of speaking anxieties that are related to a speaker's environment.

The first source is the *situation.*

The second source of speaking anxiety is the *audience.*

The third source is the *goal.*

Ways to manage these anxieties are:

**1.** *Reappraisal* – which means reframing the speaking situation as a conversation rather than a performance. It's just a conversation where you do most of the talking and your audience responds with non verbal feedback.

**2**. *Positive visualization* – means picturing a successful speaking experience in your mind. Picture yourself calm and confident. See your audience responding positively and being engaged. End with a positive affirmation – a short statement to yourself.

**3**. *Present focused-* means to focus on the present and avoid thinking about the consequences of your actions. Having a present-oriented experience, sometimes referred to as a flow experience or paying rapt attention, means you're so involved in the present that you lose track of time, external stimuli and your overall self-awareness.

Many techniques are available to become present focused:

**a**. *Being physical-* – Doing, Tai-Chi, push ups or free hand exercises immediately before a speech.

***b**. Listening to music* – Also helps to induce a present-oriented perspective.

**c.*Humour* –** Watching a funny video clip, listening to a comedy routine or engaging in a humorous exchange can also be a fun way to become present oriented.

Panic attacks

When panic starts, we stop being able to think clearly at this time. It will be helpful to be aware at this time that:

These feelings are normal bodily reactions.

They are not going to harm you.

Try not to associate with more frightening thoughts.

Tell yourself slowly what is happening.

Wait for the fears to subside!

Decide what you are going to do next

Proceed nice and slowly

Often when we begin to panic, we feel that we are "buzzing." When this happens think W.A.S.P.

**Wait** – Stop what you are doing

**Absorb** – Thing about what you are doing, and then

**Slowly**

**Proceed**

## The Dress Code

"Action is eloquence, and the eyes of the ignorant are more learned than their ears."

**-Shakespeare**

Dressing properly can enhance your personal development, help project a professional image and boost your self confidence in Public Speaking. Tests show that, personality contributes more to success than superior intelligence. Personality is the most important factor in Public Speaking increasing the power of your stage presence. Here are 10 reasons to feel more comfortable in your best attire.

1. **Authority**
2. **Credibility**
3. **Discipline**
4. Self Respect
5. Identity
6. **Individuality**
7. Power

8. **Creativity**
9. **Comfort**
10. **Visibility**

*****

## Chapter 15: The Breakthrough

Like many breakthroughs, mine occurred partly due to a degree of happy coincidence.

Firstly, as mentioned earlier, I had been thinking about the correlation between my efforts to reduce anxiety towards public speaking and the advice I had received in my meditation studies.If there is a clear understanding that by trying to stop or suppress a particular mental state you are actually **increasing** tension (not **reducing**), why was I being told that I need to relax and chill out before a public speaking engagement?

Then, one day I read a research paper by Harvard Business School's Alison Wood Brooks entitled **Get Excited: Reappraising Pre-Performance Anxiety as Excitement**.It was one of those moments where the title of this paper caught my eye while browsing the internet for research on anxiety (another book I am working on at the moment which will hopefully be out before the end of 2014).I suddenly stopped and paused and thought **"Holy cow that's it!"**

To explain why this works, let's first have a look at Ms Wood Brooks' paper.

In the first part of this study, participants were required to either sing in front of strangers or make an impromptu speech.The participants were broken into two groups in each part of the study.In the singing group, one group was required to state "I am anxious", with the other group stating "I am excited" before performing.In the speech group, the first group was required to state "I am excited" and the other group stated "I am calm".

As you probably have guessed by now, the "excited" group significantly outperformed the "calm" group or the "anxious" group.These findings were then further reinforced by a subsequent study focused on taking a (stressful) mathematics test.

My first opportunity to test this method was not a public speaking engagement, but a job interview – an event which fills me with similar levels of anticipatory anxiety! Rather than spending the preceding few days dreading the interview and trying (unsuccessfully) to calm myself down, I consciously reframed the event as a fantastic opportunity to demonstrate my capabilities in my field of expertise. I focused on the consequences of getting the job, using the expression "how exciting!" regularly.

The results were nothing short of miraculous. Not only did I spend the days leading up to the job interview free of angst, my performance in the job interview itself was excellent, as I was freed from my usual anxiety.

Yes, I got the job by the way.

The things that make **you** anxious or excited may be completely different to the things that make your friends anxious or excited. The prospect of riding on a rollercoaster at an amusement park may fill you with utter terror, while your best buddy may be beside themselves with unadulterated excitement. Why the difference?

Filters.

It is impossible for us to directly perceive the world around us. We are always experiencing life through our own particular emotional filter. And each of our filters is different, leading to a wide range of reactions to various events (such as our rollercoaster example just now).

"There is nothing either good or bad, but thinking makes it so." – William Shakespeare

William Shakespeare's famous quote perfectly captures the concept of filters and also the theoretical reason why this technique works. Rather than make futile attempts to override your body's natural reaction to a physiologically arousing event, surely it makes better sense to train yourself to view both the event itself and your body's reaction in a different way.

## Chapter 16: Wear Your Heart On Your Sleeve

It is not necessarily to reveal insights about you which may be extremely personal, and which may feel uncomfortable and painful to reveal. Indeed, this probably would not be appropriate or beneficial.

This principle is also not about revealing every little detail of your life to your audience and boring them by telling them things they do not need to know about.

However, there have been times when I have been giving a speech and, without meaning to, found myself voicing thoughts in a way that I had not expressed them before.

Wearing your heart on your sleeve is not about **attempting to come across as** being genuine, warm and sincere, but is about **actually being** genuine, warm and sincere.

For example, in an impromptu speech about work and employers, I found myself describing a group of ex-colleagues as having felt like family, and as a result, my decision to leave this job being one of the hardest I have ever had to make. As I said this to my audience, I realised that I completely meant it and felt it to be true, despite never having told this to said group of ex-colleagues in as many words. I had not made a conscious decision to reveal this detail when I began the speech, and I had not even put it into these words in my own head. I had just been focusing on delivering the speech with as much heart and honesty as I could.

The importance of devoting time to speaking off-the-cuff was addressed in the section on treating the audience as you would like to be treated. This can also tie in with the notion of wearing your heart on your sleeve (as indeed most of the different sections in this book cross over with others). This is because it can mean that what you are saying is more in keeping with your thoughts and feelings at that specific moment in time, and as a result may be more genuine and authentic.

That is not to say, of course, that prepared sections of speeches cannot be so, but for this reason, any talk can benefit from at least some sections of it being delivered impromptu. Even if a speaker makes a point of providing the audience with a lot of detail which is in line with the purpose of their talk, this is not enough if they do so in a way that is not in line with what they believe at that point in time.

Of course, if a speaker presents stories or details that are fabricated, members of the audience may well suspect that this is the case, and feel alienated as a result, or at least less inclined to listen or take them seriously.

One of the most important things, maybe even the important thing, which a speaker can do to connect with their audience, is to **be open and honest**, and show their true feelings and emotions.

## Chapter 17: It's Not What You Say

Speech content can only get you so far. Having a sincere and inspiring motivational message tucked inside your speech is like a pearl still inside its shell – hidden away from the naked eye that will adore it. Furthermore, it remains useless until it is entrusted in hallowed hands that can make it even more beautiful than it already is by letting it grow. Pearls should be worn for the world to see and not just kept. Likewise, words and messages were meant to be shared in order to create a considerable impact in one's life.

Presentation skills and performance are the factors that can take you a mile when it comes to public speaking. This aspect of your speech frees your true message and purpose. Words will remain meaningless and empty until you deliver them in such a way that will capture the hearts, minds, and souls of your audience.

Combining a substantial content with excellent speaking performance should always be a speaker's ultimate goal. Being well versed in one of them is good enough – but with the impact that public speaking has, bringing one of them to hundreds of people will not suffice. As a speaker, you don't just talk to be able to say something; you talk to be able to inspire outputs that you would like to see from your audience – you speak, ideally from the heart, to inspire change.

Did that make a difference in the way you see public speaking? I hope it did because that sets a good speaker apart from all the wannabes. If you are serious about public speaking then let's get this going.

In the past chapters we've learnt about building a superb speech content for your audience. Now, here are some tips as to how you would be able to share that marvellous content you've just created so that it'll be useful. Here are a couple of things you should remember to make the most of how you say it.

1. I know I've said in the previous chapter that beginning is always the hardest part in anything – still, this holds true for the actual speaking engagement. But like what I also said in the previous chapter, don't let that obstacle hinder you – **start your talk strong** no matter what. Projecting confidence from the moment you set foot on stage can make all the difference as to how the entire speech would go.

2. **Pace yourself** – don't go under or overtime when it comes to delivering a speech since this might become a distraction to your audience. Also, **pace your speech as well**. Don't spend too much time elaborating on something that is of little importance to the speech and the point you are making.

3. Since you're up in the spotlight, **be a little more cautious** (READ: cautious not conscious). Make sure that you maintain proper eye contact with your audience to

sustain the warmth and credibility you've established. You may also want to put much attention to your posture, gestures and facial expressions as well so as not to give out wrong non-verbal signals.

4. And lastly, **smile a lot**. It will not only ease up the tension that you're feeling within you but it will also give you a positive image in front of your audience.

Presentation Aids Or Hindrance

Getting hyped up with the last two chapters is a wonderful sign. Right about now, you are probably more interested and inspired to do public speaking performances. That's great! By now, you are also probably thinking of how to step up your game and win this challenge with a landslide. That says you're on the right track as well. Though adequate content and captivating performance are often enough to deliver a speech with flying colours, a couple of things may be added to enhance the over all experience.

Visual aids in public speaking are helpful tools in a number of ways. For one, graphics or pictures may capture and sustain the interest of the audience. Also, for highly technical topics such as those in the medical or engineering fields, slide show presentations and hand-outs can guide the audiences appropriately so that they'll be able to follow and benefit from the discussion. These materials may also be used to enhance understanding and illustrate sequences accordingly.

You must take this word of caution though. Despite the usability of visual aids in many ways, it should be made and used objectively so as to become an asset rather than a distraction to your presentation.

Keeping in mind these tips will help you produce beneficial results not only for your speech performance but for your audience as well.

1. K.I.S.S. – keep it short and simple. Do not put your entire speech, word per

word, on your slide show presentation. Doing so will eliminate the need for a speaker – in this case, you. Only include pictures, phrases or quotations that will help your audience remember key points.

2. Again, simply – verbosity and flamboyance has no space in public speaking. Keep everything thin to the bones in order not to elicit misunderstanding from your audience.

3. Make it easy – that is making it easy on the eyes and easy to see. Use fonts that are not too artsy to give a straight forward impression. Also, place them at a size that would be comfortable to the eyes of the viewers – no size 8 or 9 please! Odd colour combinations are a big no-no as well. Never use light on light or dark on dark if you want your audience to see what you've written. You may also leave the neon colours to your highlighters and post its. Always be mindful of colour contrast and combination.

Visual aids in public speaking are helpful tools in a number of ways. For one, graphics or pictures may capture and sustain the interest of the audience. Also, for highly technical topics such as those in the medical or engineering fields, slide show presentations and hand-outs can guide the audiences appropriately so that they'll be able to follow and benefit from the discussion. These materials may also be used to enhance understanding and illustrate sequences accordingly.

You must take this word of caution though. Despite the usability of visual aids in many ways, it should be made and used objectively so as to become an asset rather than a distraction to your presentation.

Keeping in mind these tips will help you produce beneficial results not only for your speech performance but for your audience as well.

1. K.I.S.S. – keep it short and simple. Do not put your entire speech, word per

word, on your slide show presentation. Doing so will eliminate the need for a speaker – in this case, you. Only include pictures, phrases or quotations that will help your audience remember key points.

2. Again, simply – verbosity and flamboyance has no space in public speaking. Keep everything thin to the bones in order not to elicit misunderstanding from your audience.

3. Make it easy – that is making it easy on the eyes and easy to see. Use fonts that are not too artsy to give a straight forward impression. Also, place them at a size that would be comfortable to the eyes of the viewers – no size 8 or 9 please! Odd colour combinations are a big no-no as well. Never use light on light or dark on dark if you want your audience to see what you've written. You may also leave the neon colours to your highlighters and post its. Always be mindful of colour contrast and combination.

4. Though you have a complete authority over your presentation, thou shall not abuse power. Make sure that every handout or slide is relevant to your topic so as not to waste your time as well as that of the audience.

5. Never rely on your visual aids to do the whole presentation for you. As its name suggest, visual aids are only that – aids or guides that will help you accomplish your goal. Remember that being independent from your visuals proves your credibility and authority as a speaker.

6. And of course, practice with your visual aids to avoid surprises during the actual performance. Doing so can also help you develop rapport with your chosen speech enhancer. Always keep in mind that speeches are supposed to be delivered as natural as possible though they are rehearsed. Being able to do so only comes with much familiarity and preparation of everything that relates to it.

## Chapter 18: How To Find The Message

Breathe Life in Your Talk
First of all, pick a topic that you genuinely are passionate about, if possible. I know there are times when you have to do a presentation that you may not be totally passionate about. In those cases, try to find something within the subject that you can believe in.

How to Find the Message
Now, let's shift to finding a message that resonates with your audience.
1. Ask yourself what are you passionate about. What are you good at?

You don't have to be a guru at the subject in order to bring out your point of view.

2. Google the subject and put forum after it. For example:

If your subject is Tennis, then you would google "Tennis Forum."

Once you are inside the forum, find the hot topic or question that needs to be answered.

3. Find articles about the specific problem within your subject.

Do not select a problem that is too broad. You want it to be specific.

Take the information from the articles and make a **basic outline** of what you want to say, taking only the best parts of your research. Remember to give credit if you are taking a direct quote from someone else.

Tell a Story

If you have any stories about you or someone else that relates put them in your speech. Keep any story short and sweet. The story is meant to back up the idea or to give a real world example.

You will notice that a lot of speeches have short stories within them.
Tell a story that highlights the facts that you are trying to make. People will remember stories much better than facts and statistics. Stories will give them a frame where to recall the message.
Whenever possible, tell a story that you've seen someone else experienced or something that you know will relate to your subject.
Big Picture Outline for Your Speech
Tell them what you will be talking about.
i.e. Today we're going to be talking about "How to Improve Your Putting in Golf."
Actually tell them
i.e. This is the body of your speech where you will actually tell them how to improve their Putting game.
Tell them what you told them

i.e. Here is where you give them a brief summary of the main points that were covered and a compelling conclusion that they can take action on.

This is not a new formula or outline. It is merely one that has worked for many people throughout time.

Practice Like a Baby

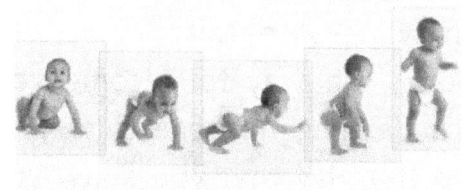

The answer to becoming good at anything is to practice. Sometimes when we become adults, we forget this.

When we were babies, we were terrible at walking. But we kept trying over and over until we got it. We practiced.

When we were babies, we were terrible at talking. But we kept trying over and over until we got it. We practiced.

That baby that kept trying is you. That baby had it all figured out until somehow through life, someone told us that falling and getting up and trying again was wrong. It's okay to fall down, but get up and try again with the same enthusiasm as you had when you were a baby trying to walk or talk.

The point that I am making here is that if we would not have accepted trying (practicing) over and over we would not know how to walk or talk.

Sooooooo, the way to become good at giving a dazzling message is to practice. Practice the way that you know you can perform and you will see that you will get better and better.

You have invested the time to know your subject, know it is time to convey understanding to your audience.

Practice, practice, practice! There is no doubt that practice can really help you deliver your message efficiently and effectively. The pressure that we will all feel once we are standing on that stage, in front of our audience, can really bring in the "butterflies" and "jelly" knees. These are all normal but are also manageable by utilizing these "tried and tested" tips:

Breathe in through your nose filling up your diaphragm and out through your mouth. You will feel your stomach fill up as you breathe in. As you breathe out through your mouth, you will feel your stomach go back down.

Organize your notes, but do not concentrate on memorizing the speech. The goal is to make sure you hit all of the important points. It's okay to hold your notes in your hand for reference as you deliver your message. You may glance at it from time to time but make sure that the delivery doesn't sound too scripted.

Use hand and body gestures naturally to accent ideas. Be dynamic by using gestures that will emphasize your message but be careful not to use distracting gestures such as nervous foot shifting, clothes clutching or hand clasping.

Consider using visual aids. However, remember to not put everything on your visuals, only the outline that will be your guide as you go through your message. Make sure the visual aids you use are large enough for everyone in the audience to see.

- If you plan on using audiovisual equipment, be sure to make arrangements to ensure the availability of the equipment that you will be need.
- Be expressive by adding variety in your tone and voice. Make your voice work for you by adjusting the pace of how you speak -- not so quick that your audience can't keep up with you or too slow that they get bored. Shift the pitch of your voice for emphasis and variety, and project your voice to all corners of the room.
- Deliver your message confidently. Confidence comes from knowing your material thoroughly; if you are sure that your speech is relevant and aimed at the right level (i.e. not too complex or too simplistic) then you will feel better about delivering it. Again, make sure to practice, practice and practice!
- End your message with a bang. This can be a "Call To Action" that tells them to do a certain thing. After the talk, your

audience should feel a sense of resolution and satisfaction.

Every time you practice, do it with the same energy that you want to have during the actual speech. Your body will remember and become accustomed to you giving that amount of energy. Your adrenaline may be pumping during your speech so this practice will help you with your pace.

The time to master your pace is during practice. You are balancing not being too fast or too slow. To hone in on your pace, record yourself. Notice if you are…

- Pronouncing your words
- Keeping your posture positive
- Delivering the speech at a good pace
- Keeping the tone conversational
- Open with your gestures, hands and body

The goal is for you to thrive through the speech, be memorable and have the audience spread the message that you have delivered to others who can benefit from it…You are reading this guide, because you know deep down that you can do it. There may come a time when you have doubts, understand that this is normal. If that happens, focus on accomplishing something that moves you towards becoming a better speaker.

**i.e.** Take a walk or close your eyes and go through the speech in your mind or just relax and do something else you enjoy.

If I can do it, you can too.

## Chapter 19: Using Slides, Images And Powerpoint

PowerPoint is a great idea for many presentations, but many presenters rely too heavily on technology and try to hide behind it. So, to help you avoid bad habits, I'm first going to warn you of how NOT to use PowerPoint.

Firstly, slides should be used to aid what YOU are saying; you should not be trying to aid or explain what is on the slide. Having one, short, punchy phrase (think Twitter kind of length) or one simple diagram is the ideal quantity of information for a slide.

Also, you do not need a slide for each idea. Instead, have a new slide for each change in section, or for every few minutes when you move on to a new topic. When it comes to how many slides you use, less is more. Ask yourself whether it is necessary to have each slide in the presentation.

Does the slide add anything substantial? Or would your presentation be much the same without it? Another danger of excessive slides is that they distract from you and what you are saying. The presentation is about your content and your idea pitch, not the content of the slides.

Having first warned of the perils of using slides, let's now look at the advantages.

Images and videos can be a great way to build an emotional connection with the audience. For example, you can talk about the need to recycle, but showing pictures of environmental damage is going to be more effective (although you may want to add a story for extra impact). "A picture speaks a thousand words." It's a famous phrase, and it's very true. You can say more through images, so it will often make sense to integrate them into your presentation. Also, using slides can help bring structure to your presentation. Using a new slide when you begin each new section will help you to pause, and it will also help clarify for the audience that you have moved on to something new.

Below are some ideas on how to make the most of a presentation using PowerPoint and similar software.

Be aware of the power of social media – choose and create lines that you think are perfect to be tweeted and put them on your slides. Make them 140 characters or less, and, if appropriate, make it easy for others to tweet and share your messages. You can also tweet them yourself and encourage others to retweet them if they can.

Use simple, natural, and clean themes in your slides. Never let the style, colours, or themes distract from the message.

Be aware of branding colours of the institution or business you are presenting at. Integrate these into borders, or text colours. Small details like this will show your attention to detail.

Don't let the software dictate how you create a presentation. For instance, PowerPoint encourages the use of bullet points. Only use bullet points if you feel that they are the best fit for what you are doing.

To facilitate some suspense and a more "physical" presentation, it can be beneficial to draw the diagrams yourself on a whiteboard or something similar. This can bring a "slow-reveal" to what you are presenting, as you fill in parts of the diagram/chart/picture, explaining each aspect as you do. Drawing something yourself will also help to bring a warmer, more organic, and inclusive feeling, as opposed to clicking through slides mechanically.

Deliver a "Call to Action"

To make your presentation more effective, it is often helpful to use a "call to action" at the end. This concept is often used in sales or copywriting. Typically, it is the final push at the end of a sales pitch to get the prospect to buy an item. Of course, not all presentations are sales-based—the final call to action in your presentation might take a variety of forms and serve a variety of functions. A call to action is important because it helps ensure that people take action on your message. For example, if you want people to recycle more, buy your product, or tell their friends about a political message, you need to ask them to do so. That "ask" is your call to action.

The call to action might look different if the goal of the presentation is less action-based. For example, if it is an informative presentation only, you might still use a call to action to make your presentation more memorable, meaningful, and informative. For example, if you want to inform people about the future of artificial intelligence, this sounds like a purely informative presentation with no room for a call to action. But you might consider saying something like, "Next time you use X device, imagine if it learned each time you used it and reacted differently over time." This call to action would help the audience leave with a memorable "take-away."

A call to action has to be a firm command, and it always contain a verb. Below are some examples to consider.

Next time you do X, why not do Y?

Buy this now to get Y benefit.

Talk to your friends about the benefits of Z.

Think about how Z might be important.

Check out website A for more details on how to do B.

Take action today if you want to take advantage of this offer.

For sales presentations, it will also help to include a sense of urgency. For example,

For a limited time only…

Take action before this deal ends tomorrow.

Buy now before the price goes up.

The call to action will be on the scale somewhere between "essential" and "possibly helpful," depending on the nature of the presentation and your goals. If it is a sales or persuasive presentation, the call to action will be essential. If it is informative, it will be less important.

## Chapter 20: Evaluation

Honesty is the Best Policy
As actors, self-evaluation is important to our success. If we can't watch ourselves perform and be critical of ourselves, we find it hard to improve as we're unaware of our mistakes from a firsthand perspective. It's the same story with public speaking.

To self-evaluate, you should record yourself speaking, either as you practice or in the real scenario (often speeches are recorded by a company anyway, so just ask for a copy!), and critically evaluate the impact you have, based on the elements covered in the first six sections of this guide.

You've done the ground-work now, but this is the most important part. There are no exercises in this section, just a guide to self-evaluation and some final tips to keep in mind.

Where Do I Start?

The self-evaluation chart on the next page has been devised so that you can break down and critique each and every aspect of your presentation skills. This allows you to identify which areas you still need to work on, so that you can go back to the relevant section of this guide and use the exercises to improve.

By marking yourself out of ten in each of the 16 areas, you are able to say, "My articulation seems fine, but I could work on my posture and gestures," and so on. This is much better than simply saying to yourself after a presentation "Well that could have been better," or listening to others saying, "You were great!"

Praise and criticism from your colleagues can be valuable, but they're likely to be biased one way or another, so watching yourself back and being honest with yourself is the best method.

Self-Evaluation

I recommend that you copy out the below table, so that you can write down your scores easily.

What the Scores Mean

Add up all the scores once you have marked yourself on everything, and you will have a number between 16 and 160.

16-64: It's likely that you lack confidence, and this is affecting your performance. By working on your weaknesses individually you can boost your overall impact and learn to effectively put on an appearance of confidence and high status.

65-126: Look at the areas where you scored 1's and 2's, and try to focus on improving them. It's likely that improvement in one area will help you to improve in others.

127-160: Congratulations, you presented excellently, and there are probably only a few things that you can improve on. Remember though, there's always room for improvement, so try not to get complacent!

| Breathing | | Breathing |
|---|---|---|
| Unregulated | /10 | Controlled |
| Shallow | /10 | Deep |
| Posture | | Posture |
| Uncomfortable | /10 | Comfortable |
| Slouched | /10 | Straight Backed |
| Stiff | /10 | Relaxed |
| Status | | Status |
| Fidgety | /10 | Calm |
| Random Gestures | /10 | Purposeful Gestures |
| Gestures Irrelevant to words | /10 | Gestures Enhanced speech |
| Vocals | | Vocals |
| Fast Speech | /10 | Well-Paced Speech |

| | | |
|---|---|---|
| Many Verbal Crutches ('uh') | /10 | Few Verbal Crutches |
| No Pauses | /10 | Well Placed Pauses |
| No Inflection / Over Inflection | /10 | Well Judged Inflection |
| Inaudible / Shouting Articulation | /10 | Appropriate Projection Articulation |
| Slurred Speech Other | /10 | Clear Voice Other |
| No Eye Contact | /10 | Good/Clear Eye Contact |
| Notes became an obstacle | /10 | Notes handled well |

A Few Final Tips...

You might be thinking, "I've got a lot to remember," after looking through the sections and exercises of this guide, but don't worry! As with everything, practice makes perfect, and the more you speak, the more you will improve. This guide is there to provide tips on how to improve quickly, from people that have benefited as performers from what the exercises teach.

There are still one or two important things to impart before you take to the podium though, and they focus on the things that are easy to forget.

These things are less about the technicalities of your performance, and more about the often overlooked things that can really enhance the overall quality of your speech.

Eye Contact

One of the most effective tools for getting your message across is eye contact. This element of nonverbal communication is a must for any prospective public speaker, and there are good and bad ways to approach it.

Firstly you don't have to stare at anyone in the audience - that wouldn't go down well. Instead, as you deliver your message, say one line to one person, then find another and say the next line to them.

Equally as important, don't rush from person to person trying to fit them all in, as that will make you look nervous. Just naturally flow from one to the next, letting the rhythm of the speech guide you.

If you are delivering your speech to just one person, for example to answer a question or to address a judge in a courtroom, give that person your full attention as you respond to them, and don't look around as though grasping for the answer. Try to stay focused.

Handling Notes

Don't become a slave to your notes, become the master of them. An audience can instantly see who's reliant on their papers and who isn't, and it effects the way they perceive you and your message. Prepare thoroughly enough that you can trust yourself not to use the notes at all, and just reference them if you need to.

The Memory section has lots of different methods for this, but it isn't always practical to learn the entirety of your speech. In that case, learn how to look up more than you look down. Even if you need your notes for the majority of the speech, don't just read them straight from the page without acknowledging your audience. Look up and make eye contact whenever you can, and don't forget to pause every now and then.

It's also important to physically hold your notes with confidence, and not shuffle through them shakily, which communicates nerves.

Picture It

A great way of countering nerves, before they even come up, is to take a moment to visualise the situation beforehand. Completely separate from physically and verbally practicing the speech, sit down, close your eyes and imagine the whole scenario, from standing up to departing. If you know the room and the audience, use that to get a good mental image, so that when the time comes, you feel like you've already done the speech well!

If you can do it in your head, it will be easier when the time comes to speak in real life. As stage performers we do this subconsciously and all the time, and it really helps to take the edge of your nerves. Be careful not to predict the audience's responses too much though, because if they end up being different to how you've planned, it could take you by surprise. On the other hand do try to imagine how you might respond to questions and interruptions!

Don't Apologise

A common trait amongst nervous speakers is unnecessary apologising. "Sorry, I'm not used to this," "Sorry, let me just check my notes," "I'm a bit nervous, sorry," "I don't know the answer to that, sorry," "Let me think, sorry."

It's much better to just get on with it. Don't say sorry for your nerves, because you'll just draw attention to them, and a lot of the time people wouldn't have noticed if you hadn't told them!

If you don't know how to respond to a comment, it's not your fault! No need to apologise, just say, "I'm not sure about that," or whatever is appropriate.

Apologising for yourself can come across like you aren't sure of yourself and your speech, so avoid it if you can.

Just Say Words

Think about what you're doing on the simplest level: standing in front of several other human beings and saying some words. Suddenly it doesn't sound so scary! Right, so the way you say the words might be slightly different from how you normally speak, but at the end of the day, you're just communicating a message.

Forget all the other stuff, like the significance of any given speech on your career, your public image, your professional life, etc. Worrying about these things will get you nowhere. Just reduce the task to what it is and it won't seem so scary.

"Just saying words" can have a more literal significance too. "Erm," "Uh," "Um," and all those other verbal crutches aren't words, so don't say them! They aren't written into your speech, and they certainly aren't going to help you get your message across!

Their Perspective

Remember that the people watching you want you to do well. If they're professional themselves, they want to understand you and listen to what you have to say. Look at it from their perspective, and think about how you perceive people when you're one of the ones listening.

Nobody is going to be as critical as you are on yourself, and nobody is going to remember a bad experience for as long as you are. If you make a mistake or speak badly, don't beat yourself up. Learn from it and move on, because the people listening probably won't care a great deal.

Just as you should imagine the scenario from your point of view, also imaging watching your speech from the eyes of someone in the crowd. It will make it a lot less scary!

Value the Experience

At the end of the day, the greatest influence on your speaking ability will be trial and error. This guide gives you the invaluable tools for technically improving your overall impact, but you can only truly learn and grow through practice.

Self-evaluation will help immensely with this, as you can quantify your performance in each aspect and see how you are improving over time. Practice might make perfect, but you will get to perfect a lot faster if you can evaluate yourself honestly and build upon your less shining aspects.

Although it sounds cliché, it really is down to you to be assertive and learn from your mistakes. There may be many lessons to learn to take you from your current ability to being how you want to be, but the first and most important one is self-awareness.

**Chapter 21: Who Is The Best Person To Organize Your Speaking Business?**

Who's The Best Person To Organize Your Speaking Business? Your guest speaker or your audience? Well, that's a million dollar question you must answer before you set out.

To organize conference related to what you know or would love to talk about, the best person to do so is you!

It's your business, and it would be a taboo to let someone else's run your business for you. It shows lack of professionalism. It shows you're not an ideal person for that business.

It's your product. It's your service. It's your information. It's your gift. It's what you know. And only you know what you know and what and what you'll love to talk about.

There is no successful businessman today who has reached that pinnacle of great success in their business by simply allowing someone else's to run their business for them!

## In This Business You Don't Need to Be A Good Orator, Neither Do You Have to Be A Skillful Writer

Alright; talking about organizing your speaking business? Maybe you're thinking, "I'm not an orator. I don't know how to speak..."

The truth is, you don't need to be an orator to go into the speaking business. Just talking about what you know, or writing on what you know or what you are passionate about on paper can do the magic.

Not all speakers are good orators; neither are they all skillful writers. If you want to find reasons not to attempt what you know you can achieve, or what can be done with your gift with little and proper training, you'll always come up with enough reasons.

But the reality still remains that there's something you know that you can talk about with so much passion and that can be set into a speaking business. Maybe your fear, assuming you're not that outspoken, can still be overcome. You can translate your passion, what you're know into a script and master you script before hand.

The beauty of this, assuming you're not a gifted speaker is that it offers the opportunity to write what you know into written form with the right words. You have the chance to read through, edit and master your speech before the day.

Remember, I said **what you know,** not **what you don't know.** And it could be what you're gifted or have passion for. With these you'll be able to describe some aspects that are connected to your gift that might not need scripting.

Alright. Look at it this way. Remember back then when you did something astounding with your gift or with what you were passionate about, and how some people asked you how you did it? How you came about with the idea?

Let me explain. Did you remember how you got so excited explaining the ideas to those who asked or who cares to know? How you described each of the processes that were involved without mincing words? And how you got so excited explaining it with so much smile and confidence?

That's the spirit! Wasn't it your idea? Wasn't it what you know and have passion for?

Why can't you do the same by organizing a conference and explaining it to excited, interested audience?

Well, that's what I'm talking about! That's what will enable you build a successful speaking business. And if you could make a little research, create an image and choose the right words for your speaking business, don't you think you will be seen as a professional speaker and even be invited to deliver speech that are related to that subject, or your interest? Or just on what you know and love doing?

The sad truth?

There is no Fairy Tale without a Dragon to Slay

Well, most people believe that to make money or to be rich through your gift and talent or with whatever you are good at you must first break your spinal cord to attain it! Not so!

There is no success that demands that you must break your spinal cord before you succeed. However, the fact that the success is your princess, and as a prince you must realized that there is "no fairy tale without a dragon to slay."

There is the real truth! You must face the dragon's teeth of disappointment, of rejection and failure. And those who have been able to face and overcome their dragon and thus rescued their princess i.e. success from the claws of the dragon i.e.

disappointment and failure are often seen and believed to be fortunate.

Look, luck or fortune has nothing to do with their success. And we all can succeed if we all are ready to rescue our princess from the dragon's den! Even if you're burn with the **firing spit of the dragon**, history will reckon with you as a hero.

So each of us can passionately say something about what we know or love and organize a seminar on it. You do it on a daily basis either with your family, friends or loved ones.

And each time you do it, you don't even know you're wasting money-making idea. You just say it and express your feeling and emotion without restricting yourself as to thought, grammar, sex or profession.

Why?

Because you know what you're talking about. You know what you know! You've been there! Is your zone! You know exactly the right phrase and the right word to use! You don't need to edit, sterilize and beg them to believe you.

In fact, if they don't believe you it makes the whole process interesting. Your adrenaline starts rushing. Your blood and creativity start pumping. You begin to crack your brain to present the argument in a most sweet, logical and concise form until you subdue them under your sledgehammer!

Ah, without any misunderstanding or misgivings, you can speak what you know to a large audience and make cool cash from it.

Probably you're now thinking, "But these people are not my family, neither are they my friends nor love bird. Some of them know more than I do. In fact, to be blunt, Joel, some of them are far knowledgeable and exposed than me?"

And so? Haven't you heard the adage that no one is an island of knowledge? You can only fret so much if you're not ready to . . .

## Conclusion

I want to leave you with this little poem.
If I'm asked for impromptu remarks, it gives my stomach impromptu upstarts.
If I'm asked for a prepared short talk, it makes my stomach grumble and squawk.
If I'm asked for a serious address, it makes my whole insides a first-class mess.
Review this report again and again. I'll bet you can go out and make a speech to any group and have fun.
I hope this information will help you gain confidence in yourself, be a better person, and help others with your great speeches.
I am available to help you personally, through email and/or skype.My speaking and coaching services are available.Plus, I can provide you with a slide show of your presentation. Let me know how I can help.

www.ingramcontent.com/pod-product-compliance
Lightning Source LLC
Chambersburg PA
CBHW072015070526
44583CB00015B/1488